Drug Addiction and Families

DATE DUE

GAYLORD			PRINTED IN U.S.A.

of related interest

Understanding Street Drugs
A Handbook of Substance Misuse for Parents, Teachers and Other Professionals
Second Edition
David Emmett and Graeme Nice
ISBN-13: 978 1 84310 351 6   ISBN-10: 1 84310 351 6

Understanding Drug Issues
A Photocopiable Resource Workbook
Second Edition
David Emmett and Graeme Nice
ISBN-13: 978 1 84310 350 9   ISBN-10: 1 84310 350 8

Cannabis and Young People
Reviewing the Evidence
Richard Jenkins
ISBN-13: 978 1 84310 398 1   ISBN-10: 1 84310 398 2

Therapeutic Communities for the Treatment of Drug Users
Edited by Barbara Rawlings and Rowdy Yates
ISBN-13: 978 1 85302 817 5   ISBN-10: 1 85302 817 7

Social Work and Disadvantage
Addressing the Roots of Stigma Through Association
Edited by Peter Burke and Jonathan Parker
ISBN-13: 978 1 84310 364 6   ISBN-10: 1 84310 364 8

Shattered Lives
Children Who Live with Courage and Dignity
Camila Batmanghelidjh
ISBN-13: 978 1 84310 434 6   ISBN-10: 1 84310 434 2

Working with Gangs and Young People
A Toolkit for Resolving Group Conflict
Jessie Feinstein and Nia Imani Kuumba
ISBN-13: 978 1 84310 447 6   ISBN-10: 1 84310 447 4

Enhancing the Well-being of Children and Families through Effective Interventions
International Evidence for Practice
Edited by Colette McAuley, Peter J. Pecora and Wendy Rose
Foreword by Maria Eagle MP
ISBN-13: 978 1 84310 116 1   ISBN-10: 1 84310 116 5

By Their Own Young Hand
Deliberate Self-harm and Suicidal Ideas in Adolescents
Keith Hawton and Karen Rodham with Emma Evans
ISBN-13: 978 1 84310 230 4   ISBN-10: 1 84310 230 7

Family Support as Reflective Practice
Edited by Pat Dolan, John Canavan and John Pinkerton
Foreword by Neil Thompson
ISBN-13: 978 1 84310 320 2   ISBN-10: 1 84310 320 6

Drug Addiction and Families

Marina Barnard

Foreword by Fergal Keane

Jessica Kingsley Publishers
London and Philadelphia

Quote from *The Amber Spyglass* by Philip Pullman on p.59 © Philip Pullman 2000. Published by Scholastic Children's Books. All rights reserved.

First published in 2007
by Jessica Kingsley Publishers
116 Pentonville Road
London N1 9JB, UK
and
400 Market Street, Suite 400
Philadelphia, PA 19106, USA

www.jkp.com

Copyright © Marina Barnard 2007
Cover illustration copyright © Jana Prchalova 2007
Foreword copyright © Fergal Keane 2007

Library of Congress Cataloging in Publication Data

Barnard, Marina, 1960-
Drug addiction and families / Marina Barnard.
   p. cm.
Includes bibliographical references and index.
ISBN-13: 978-1-84310-403-2 (pbk. : alk. paper)
ISBN-10: 1-84310-403-2 (pbk. : alk. paper) 1. Drug addicts--Family relationships. 2. Family.
3. Drug addiction. I. Title.
HV5801.B342 2007
362.29'13--dc22

2006028744

British Library Cataloguing in Publication Data
A CIP catalogue record for this book is available from the British Library

ISBN-13: 978 1 84310 403 2
ISBN-10: 1 84310 403 2

Printed and bound in Great Britain by
Athenaeum Press, Gateshead, Tyne and Wear

For Daniella, Gabriel and Rebecca

Acknowledgements

My first and largest debt of appreciation is to the many people interviewed for this book. Your names may have changed but I remember each and every one of you with deep gratitude for speaking so openly on subjects that were often painful and always close to the heart. Thanks are also due to the many practitioners who contributed to the research. Beyond this I must thank Neil McKeganey, who is always there for me. His ability to cut through to the heart of an issue unfazed by dogma and holy cows is the sign of a truly independent mind and has been a sharp spur to my own thinking. I am fortunate to have colleagues and friends like Louise Long, Andrea Bevan, Jim McIntosh, Pat Smith and Bridget Rothwell, who are always up for an incisive interrogation of the issues and who read and helpfully commented on earlier drafts. Thank you to Jana Prchalova for her wonderfully evocative book cover. Thanks also to Murdoch Rogers at the BBC for chivvying this book along during our work together on the 'Invisible Kids' Panorama documentary. A special note of gratitude is due to Steve Parkin, for so ably assisting in interviewing the grandparents. Carole Bain has my total admiration for the quality of her transcriptions. In research, access is always a bit of a sticky wicket but I am fortunate to have been given every assistance by Turning Point Scotland, the Open Door Trust, the Gallowgate and Glasgow Family Support Groups and especially the Aberlour Childcare Trust. I would like to acknowledge the support of the Scottish Executive Chief Scientist Office, the Joseph Rowntree Foundation and the Hutcheson Bequest. Lastly, I must make special mention of Joy Barlow: she was part of the research and is a dear friend, more than this, her complete commitment to children and families has been a shining beacon.

Contents

Foreword

The most common and damaging misunderstanding about drug dependancy is that it only concerns the person using the drugs. If we could just fix the addict then everything else would be alright. It is a perception which not only places enormous pressure on the individual who is dependent on drugs but it also ignores the pain experienced by families and loved ones. One of the first lessons I learned as a recovering alcoholic was that what I considered 'my' problem was in fact a problem for a lot of other people as well. The pain and illness spreads out from the addict to encompass partners, children, siblings and friends. The family can find itself caught in a web of denial, shame, anger and sheer bewilderment as the drug user is pulled away from them by the force of addiction.

Marina Barnard has written a powerful book which addresses the crisis faced by families as they attempt to cope with the effects of drug misuse. Her great skill is to blend rigorous research with keen insights and all backed up by a profound humanity. As somebody who knows something of the pain of this territory I cannot recommend her work strongly enough. She both knows and cares – a rare combination in a field where academic studies can too often forget or under-represent the human dimension.

Fergal Keane
Special Correspondent for BBC News

Chapter 1

What is the Problem?

Introduction

Problem drug use hits families like a tidal wave, leaving those involved floundering in a sea of anger, frustration, fear and isolation. Yet for all the enormity of this event, it has largely escaped notice. Drugs policy, drug research and service provision has predominantly been about meeting the needs of the individual with the drug problem, their routes into and out of problem drug use, their treatment experiences, their drug associated criminality. However, even a sideways glance at what it might be like to be the son or daughter, mother or father, brother or sister of a loved one whose drug problem takes them into danger and strife, debilitates their health and wellbeing, and leads them to steal and fight, can't help but indicate the price it exacts on families.

It is a lamentable myopia that has led to a situation where the harms that accrue to families through a close relative's drug problem remain hidden, not because they are not there to view, but because we have largely chosen not to see. In doing so we have missed the consequences that problem drug use has for others in the family. It means children who are vulnerable to a host of harms where drugs divert the parent's attention from the child; it is the burden of stress and strain for family members that often lead to ill health and depression; it is the exposure of children to drugs and the increased risks that they will themselves go on to use them. These are outcomes as significant as the developing drug problem and as demanding of attention.

Strangely, it is probably not even an intentional short-sightedness, but one arising out of the absorbing and complex dynamic of a developing drug habit with its associated problems. Family members are caught in an unfolding tragedy that rivets the family attention entirely through all its twists and turns, and the never-ending tension as to what the ending will be like. And while so engrossed, the impacts of the drug problem on all their lives are sidelined. Often it takes many years to realize that a family member's drug problem has taken centre stage. Something of this same dynamic was apparent too in the process of doing the various research projects that inform this book. Even despite carrying out research that was explicitly about the impact of problem drug use on family members, there was a propensity to miss the point, to ask more about the relative's experience of the drug problem than to ask about the ways in which it affected them. And indeed, many found it a peculiar experience to personally reflect on how they thought that the drug problem had affected them as the child of a problem drug user, or a sister or brother, or a mother or father. To further underline the point, very many of those people with drug problems found it an unusual, although not unwelcome, experience to reflect less on their drug careers than upon the ways in which drugs affected various of their family relationships. That for some drug users it was the first time they considered, out loud at least, the connections between their drug careers and the lives and wellbeing of others in their family circle, is testimony to the point that we tend to think about drugs along the narrowest of lines. These research conversations with family members are the heart of this book and, however faltering, an effort to represent the experiences of families trying to live and cope with drugs in all their lives.

There has of course been research on the family experience of problem drug use. It is, however, pretty patchy. For instance, whilst there is an increasingly authoritative body of work indicating the problems associated with parenting in the midst of a drug problem, only a fraction of research has focused on what happens when these children end up parented by their extended families, or indeed by the state. At the same time there is very little that refers to the experience of being the parent of a drug user and still less a sibling. Research interest in sibling outcomes has telescoped to a concern with whether or not they might themselves go on to develop drug problems.

The following section summarizes what the empirical evidence has to tell us on drugs in families. As I have already noted, most research attention has focused on children with problem drug-using parents. One might say on this basis that there has been no turning away from this problem; there it all is in black and white. The first point to observe is that this is predominantly US literature. There has been a very small amount of research attention paid to this problem in the UK. Undoubtedly there are similarities between the two countries, but one is not reducible to the other, given different drug cultures, ethnic mixes and policy and practice. The second point, probably related to the first, concerns the status accorded these findings and their translation into practice. The UK drug problem took off in the mid 1980s, yet it was not until 2003 that the UK government produced its first policy document, 'Hidden Harm' recognizing the needs of this group of children (ACMD 2003). It has been a long time coming. These children now number some 350,000 throughout the UK (ACMD 2003), are disproportionately represented on child protection registers and, in Scotland at least, have made up a dismal catalogue of child deaths and injuries associated with parental drug problems.

What the empirical evidence has to tell us: the impact of a drug-using family member on the family

What it is like to be the parent or sibling of a child who goes on to develop drug problems has been little explored by research and equally too, has been largely untouched by policy and practice. Looking at this, you could easily be forgiven for thinking that the impact was negligible, that families absorbed the shock and moved on, and that there was nothing that was particularly of note in this process. Yet what research there is, largely from a small team of UK researchers led by Velleman, Copello and Orford, indicates severe and enduring stress experienced by family members, which in parents can result in high levels of physical and psychological morbidity (Copello and Orford 2002; Orford *et al.* 1998a; Orford *et al.* 2001; Velleman and Templeton 2003). These families typically cope alone with the secret of their child's drug problem, often over many years, adding to family strain and distress. The playing out of problematic drug-associated behaviours such as stealing, violence, argumentativeness and unpredictability in the home have all been identified as contributing to the enduring difficulties of living with a family member who develops drug problems (Butler and Bauld 2005; Orford *et al.* 1998b).

Even here, however, the focus has been on the impact on families from the perspective and experience of parents, most usually mothers. What it is like to be the brother or sister of someone with a drug problem has been still less likely to attract research attention. In part this might be because the effects on siblings are less direct; a parent tearing her hair out with stress or suffering angina represents a more directly apprehended notion of distress than the more indirect, and usually more opaquely expressed, sense of being sidelined by the family preoccupation with trying to resolve or head off some of the problems created for and by the drug-using sibling. Family therapists interested in treating problems within a relationship context have been those most likely to call attention to changed family dynamics, to the manifestations of distress by siblings and the roles siblings can come to adopt in relation to the drug using family member (Huberty and Huberty 1986). Some parallels can be drawn outside of the field of drugs research in the small literature that has considered the experiences of brothers or sisters living in families where their siblings have chronic illnesses such as cystic fibrosis (Bluebond-Langner 1996), disability (Lamorey 1999) or mental health problems (Gerace, Camilleri and Ayres 1993). These siblings experienced parental time and energy as focused on the ailing sibling and whilst they understood this to be necessary it did not prevent them from resenting the lack of time, attention and energy available to them. The sense of a justified focus on the chronically ill child may be less easy to maintain in siblings of problem drug users because problem drug use is more often seen as a self-inflicted and therefore potentially remediable behaviour.

Parenting in the context of a drug problem

When parents use drugs, what happens to the children? What we do know is told in statistics indicating a high likelihood of neglect and abuse and poor outcomes for many, as they in turn become adults. Whilst the texture of that deprivation of a nurturing environment is missing from these various researches, they convey with some clarity the scale of the problem and are summarized below.

Problem drug use is associated with great unpredictability, both because of its illegality and because it is a chronic relapsing condition. Both facets have significant consequences for parenting children (Barnard and McKeganey 2004). The illegalities associated with problem drug use mean that children are exposed to criminality and with it to the possibility that one or both parents will be imprisoned and to the stigma associated with an illegal lifestyle. One might perhaps argue that removing the illegality might help alleviate some of these problems. However, it would not make any difference to the characteristically rollercoaster pattern of the drug career which with all its dips, dives, corners and straights defies predictability. Most parental drug careers last many years, during which their children's lives tend also to be patterned by unpredictability and frequently attendant chaos. As parents move into and out of variants of stability and chaos so do their children. During periods of relative stability (whether drug free or on a controlled dosage) the impact of parental drug use on family functioning might be minimal (Hogan and Higgins 2001). However, periods of escalating drug use quickly undermine household stability. At such times the needs of children can become secondary to those imposed by the drug problem, leaving children vulnerable (Hawley *et al.* 1995; McKeganey, Barnard and McIntosh 2002), particularly to neglect and abuse.

Physical abuse and neglect are the most common forms of maltreatment among parents who use drugs (Chaffin, Kelleher and Hollenberg 1996; Locke and Newcomb 2003; Child Welfare Information Gateway 2004).

In the US, children of parents with drug or alcohol problems are nearly three times as likely to be physically abused and more than four times as likely to be neglected than children of parents who do not have problems with these substances (Kelleher *et al.* 1994). During periods of intensive drug use by parents, children can be vulnerable to not being properly fed, clothed, supervised or cared for (Corcoran 2000; Kroll and Taylor 2003). Children's medical and dental needs are also liable to be accorded lesser priority relative to other children from socially deprived households (Cornelius *et al.* 2004). Shulman, Shapira and Hirshfield (2000) reported that 83 per cent of assessed children of parents attending methadone clinics in New York (n=100) had medical and/or nutritional disorders of varying degrees of severity which had gone unreported and had been untreated, often over many years.

The likelihood of neglect or other child maltreatment in the UK appears greater where parents use heroin (Forrester 2000). Newborns and children under three years of age are known to be at especial risk of neglect (Connell-Carrick 2003; Harwin and Forrester 2002). Toddlers were found to be the most vulnerable to abuse and neglect in a retrospective analysis by Jaudes and Ekwo (1995) of 513 in-utero drug-exposed children. Associated risk factors such as the mother's age of first childbirth and the number of children she has, as well as her psychological state and socio-economic circumstance are found to contribute to the risk of child neglect (Bernstein *et al.* 2003; Nair *et al.* 2003; Smith and Testa 2002). A further important component of these children's vulnerability lies in the high proportion of women with drug problems who are parenting alone or with serial partners who also have drug problems (Chance and Scannapieco 2002). In such cases the likely exposure of the child to the full force of the family instability must be greatly heightened.

Parental problem drug use, alongside parental misuse of alcohol is one of the most likely reasons for children being received into the care system (Child Welfare League of America 1998; Porowski, Burgdorf and Herrell 2004). This often occurs more than once (Terling 1999) and can be for lengthy periods of time (Semidei, Radel and Nolan 2001). Murphy and colleagues (1991) in reporting on cases of serious child maltreatment brought before the law courts found that parents with drug problems were the least likely to comply with court orders and that their children were the most likely to be received permanently into care.

Parent–child relationships

Although physical neglect of children has been strongly associated with parental drug use, it is also the case that drugs negatively affect the establishment of strong emotional bonds with parents (Kerwin 2005). Perhaps because emotional neglect is much less amenable to measurement than, for example, a dangerously dirty house, it is much more difficult to pin down. However, as Connell-Carrick (2003) has pointed out, physical neglect rarely comes alone, but exists alongside emotional and other forms of abuse.

Strong affective bonds with at least one parent are vitally important to the development and nurturance of infants and young children (Bowlby 1969). Infant attachment can be disrupted where parental preoccupation with drugs leads them to be inconsistently attentive, warm and responsive (Goodman, Hans and Cox 1999; Schuler *et al.* 2000). Mothers with cocaine problems, for example, were assessed as much more likely than non-drug-using mothers to be emotionally disengaged and unresponsive with their infants (Ridener Gottwald and Thurman 1994). Establishing secure attachments between babies and at least one parent is likely to be more difficult where the infant is born drug dependent and has to endure drug withdrawal once born. These babies can be irritable, resistant to being held and unresponsive to the parent, making the task of maternal bonding less than optimal.

Most research attention has focused on parent–child relationships in the early years, but parental drug problems continue to inhibit strong positive relationships with children throughout their childhoods. Kandel (1990) demonstrated, over a period of a year, an increasingly negative relationship between the severity of the drug problem and the quality of relationships that 222 parents had with children aged six and over. Increasing drug involvement in the last year was significantly associated with less supervision of the child, more punitive forms of discipline, less discussion and positive involvement with the child as well as more disagreement with partners over discipline. Mothers were particularly likely to have problems controlling their children. Similar results were reported by researchers Bauman and Dougherty (1983) and Bauman and Levine (1986) in comparing methadone-maintained women and their pre-school children with controls. The methadone-maintained mothers were more likely to parent children through negative command and were significantly less likely to display prosocial skills in parenting. Suchman and Luthar (2000) in a matched study with mothers who had opiate problems reported that low maternal involvement (a predictor of neglect) was significantly associated with problem drug use. However, inconsistent limit setting and over-control of children were better explained by contextual factors such as low socio-economic status, ethnic minority status and single parenthood. Hien and Honeyman (2000) in assessing the relationship between maternal aggression and problem drug use (primarily cocaine) found that problem drug-using mothers were significantly more likely to endorse harsher disciplinary procedures including greater use of physical punishment. Two factors predicted maternal aggression more powerfully than drug use alone: being in a violent couple and the mother's use of avoidant coping strategies.

The difficulties that many parents experience in providing safe care for their children are nowhere better illustrated than in the statistics indicating just how many end up separated from them. That less than half of all parents in England and Wales on a five-year dataset for drug misuse treatment services (ACMD 2003) were still living with their children is a shocking indictment of the impact of problem drug use on parenting. The proportion of children in statutory care was about 5 per cent; the remainder were very likely to be resident with their relatives.

The extended family

There are no reliable means of knowing just how many children from drug-affected families are living with the extended family. Partly this is because such information is neither routinely collected nor collated nationally. Partly also this is because many problem drug-using parents leave their children with the extended family on an informal basis without the knowledge of social welfare agencies (Kolar et al. 1994). The indications are however, that the numbers of children of parents who have drug problems living with relatives are substantial (Carlini-Marlatt 2005). In the US it was estimated in 1999 that 2.3 million children were being raised by a relative, most usually by a grandparent, and recent research has indicated that in most cases kinship care was assumed because of parental drug use (Chase Goodman et al. 2004).

The presumption that family is the best place for children is part of the same, often untested, belief that kin relations are beneficial and that kin networks are stable and willingly supportive (Cramer and Bell McDonald 1996). These expectations do not just operate on the social plane: they are embedded deep in the framework of social welfare systems everywhere too (Kelley 1993). However, the addition of one or, often, more children to the household can have a major impact on its functioning. Family strain, conflict and instability can all be part of the equation where another family member assumes the care of children (Caliandro and Hughes 1998; Cramer and Bell McDonald 1996). It might cause problems of overcrowding and resentment as already resident children are forced to live in cramped circumstances. Having extra mouths to feed and bodies to clothe inevitably imposes upon family resources, which can be burdensome where they are already spread thin as, for example, where relatives are out of work or living on a pension. It is also apparent from research that many of the family carers, especially grandparents, do not enjoy good health (Minkler, Roe and Price 1992; Roe *et al.* 1994) and report high levels of distress, depression and other emotional problems (Carlini-Marlatt 2005). For some families the current situation will be greatly shaped by pre-existing family problems, perhaps going back over many years, a further dimension of difficulty for everyone concerned. Furthermore, the children who come to live with them often have problems of their own, through exposure to neglect and abuse and through feelings of having been abandoned by their parent/s to be reared by someone else in the family (Chase Goodman *et al.* 2004). These factors can add greatly to the difficulties of caring for children whose anger and other negative emotions are not easy to manage and emotionally contain (Brown-Standridge 2000; Ornoy *et al.* 1996).

Faced with these disadvantages it is not surprising that many of these children develop significant problems of their own. The issue that has most dominated debate in this sphere has been their likelihood of also becoming problem drug users. The research literature is also summarized in terms of children of drug-misusing parents, and also the brothers and sisters of problem drug users.

The transmission of drug problems across and between generations

Exposure to drug misuse within the family has diverse consequences for children. On the whole it could be said that children of drug-misusing parents face a whole host of potentially negative developmental outcomes, one of which might be to develop their own problems with drugs. The siblings of problem drug users, on the other hand, appear not to experience the same range and severity of psychosocial adversity, however, they are apparently at greater relative risk of developing drug problems themselves (Boyd and Guthrie 1996; Luthar, Merikangas and Rounsaville 1993). For example, the DORIS (Drug Outcomes Research in Scotland) study, which is following the treatment careers of 1000 problem drug users in Scotland over time, shows that of the 95.2 per cent of drug users who reported having siblings, just under a third (31.2%) reported having at least one sibling who had ever had a problem with drugs and a further 8.6 per cent reported having ever had a problem with drugs and alcohol (pers. comm. Neil McKeganey 2004).

Sibling drug initiation risks

Research on the risk that a sibling will model the drug use of a brother or sister has tried to tease out the distinctive influences on their behaviour. The associations between family dysfunction (often including parental problem drug or alcohol use and childhood experiences of sexual or other abuse) have been observed in much previous research on the antecedents of problem drug use (Knisely *et al.* 2000). This leaves the question as to the relative influence of a shared family history on drug initiation, compared to an independent risk posed by an older sibling's drug use on the propensity for the younger one to try drugs. A partial answer to this might be found in Brook and colleagues (1989) work on the relative influence of a drug-using parent, elder sibling and peers on the proclivity for a younger brother to use drugs. This research indicated that older brother, parental and peer drug use each had an independent impact on a younger brother's drug use. However the degree of influence was greater from peers and older brothers than from a parent who used drugs. Duncan and colleagues (1996) drew similar conclusions in their longitudinal research on families. Although both parents and siblings contributed to the level of adolescent drug use, it was only siblings who were a significant influence in the ongoing development of the younger siblings' substance use. As 'influential friends' (Vakalahi 2001) older brothers or sisters can legitimate deviant behaviours by example (Jones and Jones 2000) or coercion (through being goaded for example) or through competitiveness. Needle and colleagues (1986) and Brook and colleagues (1983) have pointed to the important connections between older sibling and peer substance use in predicting frequency of drug use both through imitation and reinforcement. Brook and colleagues reported, for example, that 'older siblings and peer factors each had a direct effect on the younger sibling's stage of drug use' (1983, p.88).

Drug initiation risks of children of parents with drug problems

The situation for children of drug-misusing parents is more complex because their often greater exposure to psychosocial adversity in childhood can leave them vulnerable to a broader range of problems as they develop. Compared to children growing up in similar circumstances but whose parent/s do not have drug problems, these children have shown high rates of depression, anxiety and worry (Johnson, Boney and Brown 1991; Weissman *et al.* 1999). They were also more likely to be socially isolated from peers (Bauman and Dougherty 1983; Bauman and Levine 1986) assessed as aggressive, withdrawn and detached (Kandel 1990) and to have conduct problems (Silverman and Schonberg 2001). The particular link with maternal substance misuse problems and poor psychological adjust-ment of children has been highlighted in other research (Ohannessian *et al.* 2004). A growing body of evidence confirms the elevated risk that children of parents with drug and alcohol problems will develop clinically diagnosed disorders such as attention deficit hyperactivity disorder (ADHD) (Roizen, Blondis and Irwin 1996; Wilens *et al.* 2005). The children most at risk of developing psychological problems appear to be those where the parent has substance misuse problems combined with psychological problems, includ-ing ADHD (Clark *et al.* 2005; Ohannessian *et al.* 2004; Wilens *et al.* 2005).

The question as to whether or not children of parents with drug problems will follow this same trajectory is more vexing. There is research evidence of this trend (Nurco 1999), not least because such children are more likely to have friends engaged in deviance (Moss, Lynch and Hardie 2003), have access to the drugs and to be involved in criminality (Kolar *et al.* 1994). That there is no inevitable cross-generational transmission of parental substance misuse problems is perhaps best illustrated by a recently reported longitudinal study by Clark and colleagues (2005). Out of a sample of 560 children, 266 had at least a father with a drug problem, yet the majority did not themselves misuse substances throughout their adoles-cence. However, those children most likely to engage in substance use and to develop problems with drugs in later adolescence also measured high levels of psychosocial disturbance. Indeed Clark and colleagues were able to predict with some specificity which children would go on to develop sub-stance misuse problems on the basis of a devised index of psychological dysregulation. This suggests the importance of a focus on the interaction between familial, psychological and environmental risk factors in determin-ing children's pathways into problem drug use, even where they live in situations of elevated adversity.

This literature does not paint an optimistic picture. Whilst it is true that there are caveats, that there will be exceptions, the broad canvas clearly indi-cates a strong likelihood of problems and poor outcomes. The research that I will describe in the rest of the book does not offer much of a detour. As it is based upon qualitative data, however, it provides an opportunity to flesh out something of the texture of the family experience. Before doing this it is necessary to describe the research projects that informed this book.

The research studies
It is rare that one has the opportunity to consider a problem from different perspectives, rare too in qualitative research to draw on many different accounts to consider the problem of drugs in the family. This book offers

the reader a unique vantage point from which to consider the impact that drug problems have on families from the perspective of different family members. The 182 interviews that make up this book were carried out with problem drug users (meaning those who have developed habitual, most usually daily, patterns of use of illegal drugs like heroin or cocaine and its derivatives in combination with a whole host of other legal and illegal drugs and who consider that drugs are an essential feature of their functioning), with their parents, their brothers and sisters as well as with the children of problem drug users. These different standpoints offer the reader an important window into the devastation that problem drug use frequently wreaks on families. A further set of interviews and focus groups with practitioners offer the opportunity to consider how practitioners think about, and respond to, drugs in the family.

The interviews that make up this book were carried out in Glasgow, Scotland, a city notorious for the size and severity of its drug problem. Inevitably some of how drugs are experienced and responded to will be particular to Glasgow, for example problem drug users in Glasgow will typically inject and heroin will be the drug of choice (Hay *et al.* 2005). The more remarkable feature however is the thread of continuity between how these families experienced drug problems and how they have been reported to affect families elsewhere in the UK and abroad.

Three main research projects informed this book. Full ethical approval from the University of Glasgow was received for each of these studies. Participants were assured confidentiality within the confines of the Children's Act (1995) Scotland. All interviews were taped and fully transcribed with the consent of the participant. Most of the interviews took about an hour and most of those with relatives were carried out in their homes. These studies are described below whilst also providing an outline of the book's contents.

'Drugs in the Family'

The scant consideration of the experience of drug problems on close family members led to the research I shall describe in Chapters 2 to 4. 'Drugs in the Family' (Barnard 2005b) was a two-year research project, funded by the Joseph Rowntree Foundation, in which a total of 64 problem drug-using siblings, parents and siblings were interviewed: 24 had current drug problems (these are referred to as the drug-using siblings; all were aged 25 or under); 20 were parents of problem drug users and 20 were the younger brother or sister of the problem drug user. The research strategy was first to contact problem drug users and then, with their consent, to contact other members of their families. Interviewing related family members held out the prospect of a two or three-way perspective into the ways in which drugs were considered to affect the same family. This was easier said than done, but for half of the eventual sample I did manage to interview the mother (or more rarely, the father), the problem drug user and his or her sibling.

In five cases it was not possible to contact other family members, whether because the problem drug user no longer had contact with their family or because I was unable to make contact myself. Three of these problem drug users described marked family problems that precluded research contact. It is possible therefore that the eventual sample of parents and siblings was better representative of families that were more stable. Weighed against this statement, it might be added that the first point of research contact with families was through those problem drug users attending a drug crisis centre in Glasgow. As its name implies this centre has a specific remit to respond to the acute problems associated with sustaining a problem drug-using lifestyle. By definition these research participants were all experiencing severe problems in their drug careers, so there was no selection in that sense.

A small number of practitioners whose work either directly or indirectly involved problem drug users and their families were also contacted for this research. Telephone interviews were carried out with ten practitioners: two general practitioners, two head teachers, two social workers, two drug workers and two family support workers (members of self-help organiza-tions). These practitioners were asked to describe their perception of the problems faced by the family and their responses to parents and siblings. These taped and transcribed interviews were rarely longer than 30–40 minutes. Whilst clearly a very small sample, the views of these practitioners, described in Chapter 4, are worth regarding as they broadly confirm the received family impression that their needs tend to go unnoticed in the focus on finding means to assist the person with the drug problem.

'Growing up in drug dependent families'

The research that informs Chapters 5, 6, 8 and 9 derives from a Scottish Executive-funded study 'Growing up in drug dependent households' which was carried out from 1999 to 2002, with Joy Barlow (Barnard *et al.* 2000). This Glasgow-based qualitative study considered the impact of parental drug problems on children's wellbeing and welfare from the perspectives of parents (n=62), children (n=36) and practitioners (n=9 focus groups). It was based on an appreciation of how little focus there had been on the pro-cesses by which parents parented whilst on drugs, and the ways in which the children considered they were affected by their parents' drug problems. Interviewing children was particularly challenging as stigma and its associ-ated secrecy made it difficult to contact and interview children (Barnard and

Barlow 2003). It ought perhaps to be underlined that there has been a significant lack of research representing the recounted experiences of this group of children and young people.

The risks to children's psychosocial wellbeing as a result of their proximity and exposure to drugs and the effects this has on their journey through childhood are an important part of any discussion of how problem drug use plays out in families. Chapter 8 is based on interviews with 40 drug and non-drug-using siblings in the Joseph Rowntree study and the 36 children and young people who participated in the 'Growing up in drug dependent households' study.

The approach taken by practitioners in dealing with parental drug problems as they impact on child welfare and child protection forms Chapter 9. The nine focus groups convened were each made up of three or four practitioners (n=35). The focus groups were split evenly between health visitors, drug workers and social workers (three groups of each discipline).

The extended family
A critical part of the jigsaw in looking at parenting is to consider the part played by the extended family in shielding children from some of the problems associated with the drug problem (Chapter 7). This qualitative research, funded by the Hutcheson Bequest, involved 20 grandparents who had assumed full time care of their grandchildren, and one aunt. The research arose out of the study on parental drug problems, where it became apparent that the extended family played a crucial role in helping parents to parent, and in keeping the children safe.

The grandparents and aunt were contacted via two social work area teams where the children were living with their relatives under supervision or residence orders and through two Glasgow support groups set up specifically by and for relative carers.

Conclusion
Even a brief look through the literature on the effects that drug problems can have on families illustrates the extent of their reach into every important aspect of family functioning and dynamic. It sets parents against each other, antagonizes and isolates other siblings, puts children at risk and increases their likelihood of drug taking. And children of parents with drug problems face numerous obstacles to achieving even the basics needed for their safety and wellbeing. From here on the book takes its cue from interviews with many family members to tell the story of drugs in the family.

Chapter 2

Family Journeys of Discovery, Adaptation and Expulsion: Cycles of Response to Drugs in the Family

Introduction

It is hard to overstate the impact of a close family member's drug problem on the rest of the family. The discovery that a son or daughter, brother or sister has developed a drug problem leads families into a deep mire of shock, dismay, confusion, anger and sadness which it is difficult to find a way out of. And this is just the beginning: for most families the calamity produced by the advent of the drug problem deepens and intensifies through many years. This chapter documents this journey as recounted by parents, the problem drug-using family member and siblings through three stages: discovery of the drug problem; attempts to manage and live with it and the often reached effort at final expulsion of the problem drug-using relative from close contact with the family. These stages are not of course absolute or immutable, however, they generally describe the trajectories of the families interviewed here. This discussion is linked closely to the subsequent chapter, in which attention turns to considering the effects of the drug problem on family relationships and, with it, the stability and wellbeing of the family itself. Chapter 4 follows on from both chapters in considering how practitioners view the family.

As we shall see, the near daily problems brought about by the drug use of a daughter or son had enduring impacts on almost every aspect of the family's functioning. Like most people, the parents and siblings interviewed in this study on the whole had a clear sense of 'being a family', even whilst at the same time acknowledging some of the expectations wrapped up in it to be somewhat idealistic. It meant at heart that there was an expectation, even if not realized, of mutual trust, protection, love, care and support, as well as a taken for granted togetherness. The obvious exceptions to this were those family members who described markedly dysfunctional families in which they had grown up exposed to abuse and neglect and which often included accounts of severe parental alcohol or drug abuse. In this minority of five families there were no such expectations of mutual trust and affection, even whilst family members interviewed described their wish for it.

All the family members contacted in this Joseph Rowntree Foundation (JRF) study were long past the early stages of the drug problem, nonetheless it was a defining moment for most of these families in marking the distinction between a time before and after. Again, in those families where there were reports of severe and continuing dysfunction, there was perhaps less of a sense of distinctive difference, more an accumulation of adversity, as, for example, the family where a father had drug problems, and the mother and stepmother had both died of drug overdoses. Both daughters had themselves developed drug problems and these had been integrated into the overall instability of the family dynamic. For the majority of families however the difference was profound.

Just two of the problem drug users were living in the family home at the time of the research. Given an average age of 22 and a half, this might perhaps be expected. However, the great majority reported frequent, if unpredictable, contact with the family, including periods of staying at the family home, sometimes of long duration. These erratic patterns of contact were closely connected to the patterns of their drug usage: periods of relative control over drug usage might see extended contact with the family; during other, less controlled, times contact with the family might be minimal.

At the beginning

The development of a drug problem in a close family member was often an insidious process marked by small, but significant, changes in manner, behaviour and appearance (Usher, Jackson and O'Brien 2005). Perhaps surprisingly, five of these families did not realize for up to two years that drugs were behind these behaviour changes, although in nearly all these cases the drug problem had developed once their child had left the family home and was living independently. Becoming defiant, withdrawn and secretive, easily irritated and agitated, having 'funny' eyes and slurred speech, disappearing without notice, missing money and goods, were all cues that cumulatively led to the suspicion that drugs were at the heart of the behaviour changes observed:

And she was about 15. I started to see a wee change in her and I was putting it down to her age and hormones and all this. But she started just defying anything was said like 'You've got to be in at 9 o'clock'. There was no way, and you were out looking for her. Liz [sister] was always arguing with her – they shared a room. And one day she came in and 'What's wrong with you?' It was her eyes 'Nothing, I just had a wee drink mam' and I wouldn't leave it alone. But it wasn't the drink. And this continued, she would disappear and stay out all night and come back. We'd be all over the place looking for where she was but we could never find her.

(Parent: Mrs Phoenix)

Once the family became aware that there was a problem with drugs, the most likely reaction was utter panic, arising from a lack of knowledge and experience. Characteristic of the family response at this time was the impulse to resolve the problem internally by recourse to family resources. Typically, parents would underestimate the degree to which their child was able, or wanted, to break free of drugs and overestimate their own capacity to bring this about. Families found it extremely difficult to come to terms with the single-minded focus on getting and using drugs and the drive to meet this need at seemingly any cost. Witnessing the physical, social and emotional changes to sons and daughters, who became thin and drawn, unyieldingly argumentative and apparently self-obsessed, produced in many parents an impotent rage and acute sense of their powerlessness to halt the unfolding pattern of family tragedy:

I: What's the worst thing about drugs for you?

R: The destruction it does to your family and the destruction it does to yourself. I always say drugs took me to places that I didn't want to go to, you know, mentally, physically and spiritually. They're a killer, even for the families and for the people that's looking on, I think sometimes we're in the worse place than sometimes what the drug addict is, because you feel so powerless, there's not a thing you can do.

(Parent: Mrs Cameron)

For the most part, parents floundered out of their depth, without any real idea as to how to help their child, but hoping that their authority as parents and their strength as a family would help their son or daughter come through it. They drew on their capital as authoritative, caring and protective to try to influence their child's behaviour. In the ensuing battle of wills, the drugs would usually win out, leaving parents under no illusions as to the power of what they and their child were up against:

> I mean we locked him in his room and everything. We'd like locks on the bedroom doors. They were climbing out windows. We'd actually put the bars, them with slats right across the…and my doctor says to us, 'em… 'They're going to have to want to do it theirself – doesn't matter how long you keep them in there, as soon as they go back out, they're going to have to want to do this theirself.'
>
> (Parent: Mrs McTavish)

The following account mirrors this struggle between the will of the parents and that of the child becoming locked into a drug habit. As this problem drug user acknowledges, even submitting to being locked in could not prevent his continued use of drugs:

> I took heroin when I was younger, about 15, once, then but when I started using it regularly at 17, it wasn't long before I lost it and it took everything away from me, you know? My heart, my soul, everything. And to a point I broke down and just says to her 'Ma, I need help' and they tried to lock me in the house and like help me to get off it and all that. But they couldn't do that because if I wanted out I'd get out, you know: 'I feel better the day' and all that and, just act, you know.
>
> (Problem drug-using sibling: Matt)

The most likely external source of help, if sought at all, was the family general practitioner (GP). As one parent stated, it was at this time, before her son's drug problem became really entrenched, that she might have been able to help him most, had there been any guidance and support for them as a family:

> It just seemed to spiral kind of out of control, you know what I mean. I've always said that if somebody had says to me in the beginning. I think I might have been able to do something; I might have been able to put a stop to it.
>
> (Parent: Mrs Smith)

However, for many families their sense of shame precluded seeking help from outside of their closest family relatives. This circle would exclude even the extended family for some, at least in the early days. Clearly the burden of carrying such a secret would have added greatly to the strains felt by the family.

It is predictable that the family response would be to concentrate attention upon the child with the problem, to try to sort it out and bring that
child safely back into the fold. The realization of the intractability of their
child's problem and their limited capacity to alter its course marked a new
understanding that this might be their family situation for the foreseeable
future. Whilst still holding out hope, and usually too, the offer to help their
child to stop using drugs, families would at some level adapt to this new
reality by trying to manage and contain the drug-associated damage. The
effect this had on family dynamics is considered in the following section,
which encompasses this second stage of family adaptation to the drug
problem.

Living with the drug problem

Living in close proximity to a son or daughter, brother or sister with a drug
problem is akin to living in the eye of a storm:

> Drugs…it destroys a family, so it does. I mean…it destroys their parents'
> life. It can split them up. You know, the weans [children] suffer, the grand
> weans suffer terrible because they've no' got their parents any more and
> the grandparents suffer all the time because it's their weans that are on
> drugs and it's their weans that are coming into their house and stealing
> off them right, left and centre, you know and it's just…it's…it's just like
> a spiral thing, I mean it just goes round and round all the time, you
> know?
>
> (Parent: Mrs Blackie)

Most families attested to the destructive power of drugs and one mother
described it as 'the end of relationships'. Yet, because there was, at least at
this stage, a strong feeling of obligation to continue to help and support the
family member with the drug problem, the response of most families was to
attempt to find some means of coping with the onslaught of problems
brought by the drugs. Typically this would involve an at least minimal
acceptance that their child had a problem that they could perhaps minimize
through its accommodation within the family dynamic. Keeping the child
safe from harm was a prime concern and it was to this end that they would
try to contain the damage, usually through keeping the child within the
family environment as much as possible. This way at least they could hope
to limit their involvement in the drug world and perhaps avoid the associated dangers of infection and harm, of criminality and violence. However,
this accommodation exacted a heavy toll on the family. The ideal of the
family pulling together was greatly strained by the sheer number of

problems brought in the wake of the drug habit and the differing responses of family members to them. This can clearly be heard in the following account by a mother still trying to adjust to the death of her son through overdose and her struggle to contain a sense of resentment that in turning away from him, the rest of the family was at some level culpable:

> I was very angry with them [his brothers and sisters], very resentful towards them. It works both ways because they become very resentful towards you. But I would say it took a long time after he died, I can see their side now, aye, they were angry. I still don't think as if he deserved to be treated in that way because he wasn't someone who broke into houses or stole off people, he was just harming himself really and in harming himself he was affecting the whole family...everyone's emotions are all shot up...

(Parent: Mrs Garvey)

In trying to prevent harm, some parents reported an uneasy involvement in funding their child's drug habit; in paying off drug dealers and debtors; sometimes allowing them to inject drugs in the home so as to reduce the risk of overdose or shared needles and sometimes, too, purchasing the drugs for them to alleviate withdrawal symptoms. This was not a role they had envisaged for themselves, but one that could develop through trying to prevent some of the accruing harms associated with an illegal, dangerous and expensive drug habit. Some parents, in looking back, were frankly amazed at the place that their child's drug problem had taken them to:

> I mean at one point I could have been in the jail myself just now. My sister and I had to go and lift the mother off the streets in the town because when Damien [mother's son] was in the jail she was dealing heroin to feed herself. So she used so much of the dealer's heroin and she'd got into debt with it. So Dave [mother's husband] had given me money to go and clear the debt because Damien was getting out the jail and he was the one to cop it because she had got into such a debt with the stuff she had used. But they [dealers] were going after him. So he got out the jail and Dave gave me £200 to go down and pay this heroin dealer off. Plus I had ten bags o' heroin in ma pocket that she...honest to god, that she had in her pocket...and I was walking about the town wi' these ten bags o' heroin in my pocket and this money to pay this drug dealer off.

(Parent: Mrs Lennie)

Although most families at this stage had, to a degree, come to terms with the reality of the problem they would still be very concerned to limit public knowledge of their child's drug habit. This appeared to arise out of a desire to protect their child, as well as the rest of the family, from public censure. The stigma associated with problem drug use is pervasively tainting of families:

I: Is it shameful for you?

R: It is, they do because some of the times she's went in and she's stole other people's kids toys and they come up and say 'She stole out the house.' And you go out and you feel it, you see the heads going and maybe you'll walk up and they're going on 'Aw see these f'ing junkies. The bane of our life.' And you're standing behind the person who's doing all the talking and the other one's trying to go… You know they're trying to say 'His mother's standing there.'

(Parent: Mrs Nugent)

As is evident from Mrs Nugent's account above, the likelihood of maintaining the family front, in the face of such behaviours as stealing from the community, is not high. Other behaviours such as abusive shouting in the street or being evidently incapacitated in public, brought embarrassment and shame:

We got invited to weddings…you know, family affairs and that and they [sons] would get turned out for that under dire threat, you know, to behave themselves, not to be looking drunk or full of it and then of course we would be half way through the night and they'd been to the toilet a few times and suddenly they were fucking stoned out their boxes, you know, and it was that, all that kind of pressure and all.

(Parent: Mr Merrick)

However, despite these public displays and, with it, the community knowledge of problem drug use, many families would shy away from public affirmation of their child's drug problem, and as in the following case would avoid involving even the extended family:

'Cos my ma doesn't know much. I never ever spoke to anybody about Ben, never. It's only this year, and you can ask anybody, never once did I ever mention Ben to anybody, or the drugs, or anything. I, I was just too embarrassed, that was all. Never ever, I think that's… I think for ten year it was just all building up inside me 'cos I never spoke to anybody. If you'd says to me, even if I'd known you for years and you says to me 'is your Ben a drug addict?' I'd have, I'd have put you out the door. 'That's my boy you're talking about', you know what I mean. 'There's the door'.

I would put you out the door. I wouldn't have let you say anything against him. Even although I knew. And at, at the back of my mind I knew that everybody else knew – but they weren't getting it from me. You would never have got me saying 'my boy's a drug addict'.

(Parent: Mrs Smith)

This shame and embarrassment could, and did, lock families into isolation and deepening distress.

Considering theft from the home: one aspect of the problem

To give a sense of the family dysfunction associated with the problem drug use we can focus on one aspect of the problem, the very commonly reported theft of goods and money from the family home to buy drugs. There is of course the inconvenience of the theft to consider, but the damage was far greater than could be measured in material terms.

In this study, persistent theft from the family home was reported by a majority (19/24) of the problem drug users. Parents and siblings were often frankly amazed by the volume and speed with which things disappeared from the home:

We used to have a massive, massive CD collection…that was my pride and joy. And…we noticed it was going down and going down and then I noticed…like gift sets out the toilet or my dear perfumes and that going out the room, bits of my jewellery…

(Parent: Mrs McTavish)

Seemingly anything and everything could be sold to buy drugs. Younger siblings' piggy banks went missing, so did clothes, jewellery, food from the freezer and toiletries. As one mother wryly put it:

If they sold blood here I think if I went to sleep at night, if I ever got up in the morning, I don't how many pints of blood they would take out your arm, they'd be away selling my blood.

(Parent: Mrs James)

Those families where the family member with the drug problem habitually stole from the house literally described it in terms of predation. Bank accounts were emptied and pension books were stolen, even at the price of leaving the parent without money themselves:

I went to get my pension book in my bag, which I left in my bag, and there was no pension book and he got it cashed in Easterhouse and I

> phoned him [son with drug problem] from my work and whenever I
> came in, he was sitting crying and he had fifteen pound left of my
> pension.
>
> (Parent: Mrs McCall)

This mother's son was full of remorse for having stolen her means of
income, as was the following son whose urgent need for money had led to
him ripping his mother's gold chain from her neck:

> I've tried to contact her but I've seen her up in Duke Street and that and I
> just walk by and she just walks by 'know? I seen her and I just looked
> away the other way and that. It's because I'm ashamed at what I done
> because I actually grabbed at her neck because I was pure strung out
> [drug withdrawals] d'you know what I mean? And she wouldn't give me
> any money and that's why I grabbed the chain.
>
> (Problem drug-using sibling: Hunter)

A parent's refusal to provide money could provoke verbal abuse, which in
public was degrading, as a drug user's sister describes:

> He was just total…evil and he thought he was always right and he never
> ever…he just, once an argument started he would never back down
> from it. Like even when my mum had…he would go to my mum 'shut
> up' and then it would get to the stage he would actually lose it, shout and
> bawl. If my mum went like that, 'right, just get out the house' he would
> shout the whole way down the close [tenement stairwell]…and the
> whole way down the street he'd be shouting 'ya fucking bitch'
> and…know, name calling and whatever. So…
>
> (Sibling: Martina)

It was not just humiliating, but hurtful and upsetting to be at the receiving
end of such tirades, even if it was understood that it was the need for drugs
that was fuelling their behaviour:

> R: Like…she'd start screaming at you, you know? …I mean she said
> some very horrible names, abusive things to you, that I couldn't believe
> they come out of her, you know? Things like 'I hope you die of cancer'
> and 'I hope you've got this, I hope you've got that' and if…
>
> I: Why would she start doing that, saying all that?
>
> R: Just coming off the drugs and not having the money to…she'd want
> to borrow five pound off you, ten pound and you're saying 'no'. Or she
> would appear – when she didn't live here, she'd appear at the door,

'em… 'I need…going to let me in for five, ten minutes' and I'd let her in and then she'd 'can I get the bus fare, can I get this' and I said 'I'm not giving you nothing' and then she would start, it was like horrible…it wasn't even swearing at you, it was just horrible things that was coming out her mouth. Horrible things.

(Parent: Mrs Smart)

The cost of these behaviours was far greater than could be measured in pounds, shillings and pence. The greater price was exacted in the degradation of family relationships, in the loss of trust and respect. It meant that nothing was taken at face value, even a statement of affection was apt to be interpreted as manipulative:

It's always money, money, money. And I mean it makes me cringe when he puts his arm round me and he'll say 'I love you Ma' and I push him away because I know it's not genuine… And it's terrible to do that with…but I can't help it… And that was the reason I was giving him money, I couldn't cope with him because he kept on and on and on and on.

(Parent: Mrs Blane)

It was not that drug-using family members did not feel sorrow, remorse or shame for their raids on the family. However, these feelings might not be enough to prevent their repetition, the needs imposed by the drug habit could be more compelling. This single-minded predation on family resources that was experienced by most of the families interviewed was considered a deplorable derogation of the role of trusted family member. Something of this can be heard in this sister's comment on the effects on her parents upon returning from holiday to find that their son had stolen all their cash in the house, fraudulently used their credit card and crashed their car:

He just doesn't know how much damage it does, know what I mean? He has no idea. 'Cos he's not seen it, 'cos he's never there to see all that part; he's always away spending it or…like avoiding us basically. He's never there to see it, know what I mean, how much damage it actually does.

(Sibling: Martina)

Some parents reported that rather than have credit or debit cards, which were often targeted, they had no option but to live with the inconvenience of having to visit the bank in person each time they wanted cash. And still they would be vulnerable to theft, sometimes through ingenious foils:

One day we got a letter from the bank, know, looked through the bank statement and went…and by this time we'd no…no pin number, cards lying about, no nothing. Nothing. And still there was about three or four hundred out the bank again. I went away up to the bank and I… And em…she [bank clerk] says 'well, it's the mandate…your daughter took out' and I'm like 'what mandate?'. She says that, she'd signed all the papers; she'd signed my husband's name. She [daughter] went up and says that her dad…was no longer able to go the bank; she'd have to do his business for him. She must have been so plausible, must have been.

(Parent: Mrs Smart)

As this parent, like others, went on to explain, the only real route to recovering the money was to involve police and have their child legally charged with fraud. However, to do so was so humiliating and shameful and so far at odds with their notion of being a family, that most parents would resist this course of action.

Losing trust in a drug-using child or sibling meant that families had to adopt hypervigilance in the home to protect money and goods. Often this resulted in an exacting routine of surveillance and resultant angry clashes as family members followed their movements into and out of rooms to try to ensure that there was no theft:

'What are you doing'… She always says 'what are you doing following me, can you not trust me' or something like that and she's always, she's always blaming it on you when it's always herself…because when she's coming in and she's doing stuff, like trying to steal stuff and all that and it just makes your head just…when you could be doing something else, it just makes your head really sore and you just feel knackered.

(Sibling: Danielle)

Nothing about this situation sits easily with the commonly held ideal of the family home as a place of some respite and relaxation. Having locks placed on doors to bedrooms and hiding valuables away, monitoring behaviour and assuming always the worst of your child or sibling was deeply at odds with this notion. As a site of endemic conflict the home became, for many, a source of distress, rather than respite from the outside world.

The perceived lies and deceits, claims and counter claims were exhausting and created a climate of endemic distrust. The person with the drug problem would be blamed for losses and disappearances and these accusations would be met by outright denial. As both parents and siblings pointed out, however, it was not always the case that the drug-using family member was responsible for the missing object, things did go missing because they were genuinely lost. The presumption however, based on past experience, would be of theft:

> I mean I've got to be honest, I hide things yet, and I go to get them and I can't find them and I'm going 'Oh dear God' (laughs), but I'll hunt and hunt before I'll say anything to him because if you say anything he goes mental. Because I'd money in an envelope one night and I couldn't find it anywhere and I says to him 'Did you see...' 'Oh here we go again, here we go again'. I got the money but I says to him, I says 'Right I've got it, okay'. 'No, but you thought I'd stole it.'

> (Parent: Mrs McNabb)

These homes were battlegrounds, where skirmishes frequently erupted over the real or suspected incursions of the drug-using family member who was almost invariably blamed for family conflicts and problems. One can see that even just considering the commonly experienced problem of theft indicates a spiralling capacity for severe and enduring stress that was deeply divisive and strained family relations often to breaking point.

The next and final section of this chapter discusses the point reached by most of these families where they considered that the costs of attempting to contain the damage were simply too great, resulting in efforts to expel the problem drug-using family member from the home.

Tough love: exclusion

> But throughout the years you keep fighting it, you're fighting a losing battle. Because you want, you're determined to get your daughter back, get that person back. ... That person's gone, they don't exist anymore and the only thing you can do is to get tough, what they call 'tough love'. So you have to...I think that was the killer; that was really the hardest part. Because it kills you, a part of you dies because you've got to steel yourself, you've got to practically be a bitch, really be a bitch, harden yourself, turn your back, leave them as dead.

> (Parent: Mrs James)

To cut adrift a son or daughter, brother or sister, fully in the knowledge that to do so will increase their vulnerability to all manner of adversity, is an enormous step for a family to take. Yet in the face of the damage to the family caused by trying to contain and manage the drug problem over many long years, it was a step that most of these families had taken. Parents spoke literally of the stark choice they made for the survival of families they had come to see as traumatized and damaged by the frequent incursions of the drug problem into all their lives. Alongside this was the growing under-standing of their limited ability to change things for their children. The following mother's decision to curtail the contact between her drug-using daughter and the rest of her family was based on the judgement that she had done as much as she could do and she had a responsibility to give her young sons a chance:

> I said I'm going to see to the boys, I'm going to give them a wee chance and they're not going to get brought up with all this bedlam…

> (Parent: Mrs Connelly)

When families reached the point where they felt that they could no longer continue to retain this central focus on the relative with the drug problem, they typically would try to institute rules of engagement. These would usually entail limiting the access of the drug-using family member to the home as a means of preventing stealing and forestalling more conflict. Also, parents would try to refuse any further provision of money. It was with a heavy heart, a sense of having failed as a parent and deep-seated anxiety as to the fate of the child that these decisions were taken. One gets a sense of the resolve required from this mother's account of her son Richard's arrival at her door in the early hours of the morning, with his pregnant girlfriend, and nowhere else to go:

> I went 'you're not getting back in this house again'. I says 'I've got Donna and Dean' [younger children], I says, 'these two, their nerves are shattered' I says 'for the age of them' …when I went to the window the rain was stoating [pouring]… Stan [stepfather]…gets his boots and he went 'I'm going to get him' – because of the state I was in, because I turned him away, and I went 'don't, just leave him, leave him' and that's when I, sort of, I gained respect from Richard.

> (Parent: Mrs Tavish)

The institution of family rules was a significant turning point for these families, marking a shift towards considering the effects of their child's drug problem on the rest of the family. However, these rules were not immutable, it was not always possible, or desirable, to keep the drug-using relative at arm's length. Where there were signs of recovery from drugs, the family would usually rally to support; when they were ill they would often be taken home and a death or birth in the family would bring them all together. It was however, something of a revolving door arrangement, as transgressions would result in expulsion.

We've tried and we've tried. Every time she's tried to get herself back up we've been there for her, we've helped her get her house furnished again, we've helped her with everything basically, and then she's just…you think maybe this time she's going to…it's going to happen this time, maybe. You get all your hopes built up, you see her making an effort with Brianna [her daughter] and then one day she just doesn't turn up and that'll be it for months upon months.

(Parent: Mrs Young)

The most difficult aspect of refusing any longer to take a lead role in protecting and caring for their sons and daughters with drug problems lay in the possibility of exposing them to greater danger. It was to try to avoid overdose that parents had allowed their children to use drugs in the house, it was to avoid their involvement in criminal activity that they had given them money to buy drugs. In withdrawing this help, parents knew that they reduced the choices open to their children and their vulnerability to such outcomes. The knock on the door was their greatest fear:

Two detectives came to my door a few weeks ago and they chapped [knocked on] the door and they went 'can you let me in, it's CID', and I fell against the wall… See when they says 'CID', either she'd done something really bad or she was dead…when Amanda's drug taking, see your phone? You're feart [afraid] to answer your phone, you're feart to go to the door, that's the way you're living.

(Parent: Mrs Leeson)

Brothers and sisters fretted over the dangers their siblings were exposed to:

I always think about them, there was never a night when I went to my bed when I didn't think about them, one away full of it [on drugs], what could happen, if he would overdose and be found somewhere and the other [brother in the army] maybe a bomb would explode on his head.

(Sibling: Simon)

Aside from the ever-present worry as to what might be the situation of their sibling or child, it was clear that home was a less stressful place when they were not present. Everybody could relax their guard a little, there were fewer minefields to negotiate and, in a more predictable environment, it was possible to find some measure of stability and routine:

Sometimes you feel like people are wishing that she wouldn't come back. Not in a bad way but it's just a lot easier for people when she's not about.

(Sibling: Nick)

Although not usual in these data, there were parents who tried completely to sever their links with their son or daughter. One mother had in fact obtained a court injunction to prevent her son from coming near her on account of the severe harassment occasioned by him. For the most part though, parents and siblings continued to try to maintain some contact and be supportive but finally at arm's length, in an attempt to reduce the negative impacts on the rest of the family.

Conclusion

The train of events set in place by the development of a close family member's drug problem profoundly affects every member of the family and every aspect of family life. The family shock on discovering the drug problem, the inability to alter its course and the ensuing onslaught of associated problems resulted in deeply disturbed family structures and dynamics. That these families were very largely coping alone, even despite the great strains imposed on them, indicates the importance of initiatives that might help families come to terms with, and respond to, their child's drug problem and its effects on them all.

The next chapter is closely related to the stages of family response to the drug problem as it considers the ways in which family relationships are affected by the drug use of one of its members.

Chapter 3

Distorted Roles
and Strained Relationships

Introduction

It should be obvious from the previous chapter that the developing drug problem has serious and compounding problems for every member of the close family, usually spanning many years. The family effort to contain and manage the drug problem was predictably played out in the constellation of family roles. What the majority of families described was a situation where their family member's drug problem became the axis around which the family dynamic would revolve. The troubles created by the advent of a drug problem would escalate, absorbing time, energy and every other resource, as parents and siblings attempted to cope with, and limit, the accumulating damage. Inevitably, parental and sibling roles across and between generations were significantly affected by the unfolding pattern of events associated with their son's or daughter's, brother's or sister's drug problem, and it is to this issue that this chapter turns.

The distortion of family roles

The process of family adaptation to the drug problem appeared to be one of trying to meet the needs of the drug-affected child in the family home whilst also trying to maintain the family. These needs were very often at odds with each other and a source of great conflict and role strain. With the family focus so firmly on the problem drug user there was little room left for the maintenance and revitalization of other relationships, whether between parents, between parents and siblings or between siblings. Furthermore, the ongoing onslaught of problems associated with the drug problem continually undermined efforts to find some family stability. This volatility was unsettling and added to the disagreements among family members over how best to respond.

The enormous strains of trying to cope with problem drug use are indicated in the following interview extract, in which a father makes plain this sense of a family besieged by effects of living with two sons with drug problems:

> I would go to work and come back and they'd be stoned and…we got into the old routine, ye know, that, 'eh, they would swear blind to their ma they hadn't took anything and I knew they had. And me and her would be fighting and they two would be in the room laughing up their sleeves… Or they would steal something out the house…and that was causing more fucking hassle, you know, it wasn't just stealing off us, they were stealing off their brothers. You'd buy them new training shoes and they'd disappear the next day, so it was all that, you know, chaotic stuff was happening… She couldn't talk to me and I couldn't talk to her about it 'cos I got angry and you know, I'd end up fucking smacking one of them so she wouldn't say too much, you know. We tiptoed about each other when we weren't arguing and our whole life had went to fuck. I was neglecting the other two boys that never took drugs, you know, I was neglecting the whole family. I was putting money in, I was handing in my money into the wife and that, but I mean that was about it, I wasn't doing anything else.

(Parent: Mr Merrick)

Here is a family turned upside down and at war with itself. The parents are divided in their response to their two boys with drug problems, with the mother shielding the two boys with the drug problem, covering up their transgressions, and defending them from the wrath of the father. The father's inability to cope with the stress led him to avoid being in the family home, one effect of which was that the other two boys were not getting much in the way of attention. The house was reeling under the strains of the stealing and all the attendant arguments and conflict. Having more than one child with a drug problem would undoubtedly magnify the intensity of the problem, however, these same elements were present in every account provided by parents and siblings with a problem drug user in the family. And because problem drug-using careers tend to last many years, the family had little choice but to adapt to this chronic state of affairs.

Relations between parents

In an ideal scenario mothers and fathers would jointly agree a plan of action in responding to a family problem. However there was little evidence of this in these data. On the whole, mothers and fathers appeared to hold conflicting views as to how to respond. Mothers were more likely to emphasize their responsibilities to their children, even despite the costs to themselves:

> I think mother and…you can't break that bond. I mean other than that Ashley [daughter with drug problem] wouldn't be here entirely, you know what I mean? You wish you could cut, at times you wish you could…sever that… If that was a…a neighbour, a friend, a cousin, an acquaintance, you could easily say 'oh, pfff, away you go, I don't want to see you again' but you can't do that. As a mother, you…can't cut it, you know?
>
> (Parent: Mrs Smart)

In light of this, they would therefore often pursue a course of action that kept the child as close to them as possible, in the hope that it would enable them some control over the situation. In this enabling role they wanted to sort it out for their children; to stop their drug use if they could and, if not, to protect them from harm. Fathers were apparently more sceptical of the merits of this strategy. These data do not allow categorical interpretation of fathers' responses as few (2/20) volunteered for interview. Partial insight can be gained from interviews with the mothers who described their sense of their partner's response to the child with the drug problem. They appeared more inclined to exclude the child from the home in an effort to stem this damage. Such divergence in parental views as to how to respond greatly strained parental relations:

> I shut off and I just wouldn't…I didn't see them from fucking week to week, I just wouldn't go in the room to see them even, you know… The first year or two it was…they weren't my boys, they were hers, know what I mean, they were her boys.
>
> (Parent: Mr Merrick)

The interviews with mothers suggested that this effort of fathers to cope through distancing themselves from the child with the problem, and indeed from the family, was not an uncommon response:

> Basically Andrea's dad went into denial and it was quite a few years before my husband actually recognized that my daughter was a drug addict. …So my daughter was manipulating the situation, saying a lot of this is in my mind and my imagination about it. It had come to a point where I began to question myself and think, 'Am I really making too much out of it?' But my logic always came back and I knew. There was a point where it could have been make or break for us because it was coming to that point where I was like 'Well if you're not going to

recognize these issues; I can't cope with her and cope with you not recognizing it.'

(Parent: Mrs Miekle)

It was rare to find families in which the birth parents were still living together (4/24); the most likely scenario was that there had been parental separation and later reconstitution of the family with one, or serial, stepparents. Disagreement between birth parents and step-parents over the child was apt to coalesce around these fault lines and added to the discord:

> He used Leah and Leah used him to bounce off me, and I knew all this was happening, and trying to juggle it, and then coping with the kids at the same time.

(Parent: Mrs Connelly)

Reconstituted or not, however, the parents interviewed reported high levels of severe and persistent discord between them over how to respond to the child with the drug problem and the costs to the family as a whole.

Mothers as mediators

Lacking agreement over how they should respond, many of the mothers described how they hid their son's or daughter's transgressions from their partners, and indeed the rest of the family in an effort to avoid any increase in conflict:

> I think when you're a mother, you know you say things and it's very hard to turn away. Very hard you know, to give up on her. I mean he [husband] just can't cope, can't cope with it at all. He doesn't sleep and he worries with the result that apart from… I had to tell him with Mia [grandchild, taken into care for neglect], I didn't tell half the things that went on. He didn't know. I tried to keep as much from him.

(Parent: Mrs Cairns)

Mothers would reportedly provide food and money surreptitiously to their drug-using children when they were not supposed to come to the house, or replace stolen goods, as in the following account, where in order to prevent the eruption of another major argument, the mother went out looking for her son's new leather jacket that his sister had just stolen:

> I says 'You better get that off or I'm phoning the polis [police], she's taken that from the house.' It was her boyfriend. I said 'You better get that off.' My boy doesn't know from this day that they were taken. Do

you know what I mean? I was terrified to tell him because he would have killed her.

(Parent: Mrs Robertson)

The mother's efforts to mediate between the child with the drug problem and the rest of the family left her isolated midway, typified by the following mother's comment 'I was trying to keep everybody the 'gether. I was trying to keep everybody happy'. The price exacted for this brokering role was stress. Indeed very many of the parents reported stress-related illnesses such as angina that were attributed to the development of their child's drug problem. For this mother it was all finally too much:

He got the last 20 pound I had and I had to borrow money off my sister to keep me going and I thought I can't go on like this because I'm hiding it from the boys and you're just a constant wreck in case he comes to the door demanding money while they're in, and all this big hullabaloo and, you know, I just…I couldn't cope, I really couldn't cope.

(Parent: Mrs Thomson)

In taking on this role of shielding the child with the drug problem from other members of the family, these mothers recognized they were engaged in an often hopelessly delicate balancing act. Trying to keep both sides happy was rarely feasible and was a further source of dissension, particularly as other siblings felt that the family was being manipulated and, in the process, they were being pushed to one side:

My brothers have slept rough and that but they've always had somewhere, they always know they can come to my ma's and my ma will open the door and say, 'come on in' and that to me is really annoying. I'm like that to my ma, 'they're just ripping the pish out of you, go and use drugs for a couple a weeks, turn up here, they feel sorry for theirself for a couple a days, stay here for maybe a fortnight', I says, 'and then, as soon as they get their giro [social security payment] or their book or whatever, they just fuck off again'. She says, 'What am I meant to do? It's my sons.' And I say 'but what about me? I'm your son and you push me to the side for them'. 'No I don't', 'aye ye do', 'no I don't'.

(Sibling: Martin)

Where other family members became aware that their mother was hiding things from them or, to their minds, showing disproportionate care and attention to their brother or sister with the drug problem, it was prone to be interpreted as favouritism and was a source of discord.

Divided parental attention

Parents spoke of how their other children were inadvertently pushed aside in their preoccupation with trying to help the affected child, even whilst they might not have seen it at the time.

> My whole life, every minute, every day of my life, revolved round Jenna [daughter with drug problem]. …And see in all honesty, Brandon [son] did get pushed to the side… And you know how you know you're doing something but…and you know it's wrong, but you still continue to do it?… But I was so focused on her all the time because she was the one that had the problems, she was the one that was…that's life was getting ruined. Her wean's life was getting ruined and I felt that Brandon was getting looked after…and I thought 'Brandon's alright' but is he really alright?
>
> (Parent: Mrs Blackie)

It is worth underlining that the drug problems of their older brothers and sisters had developed when most were still quite young children and correspondingly more in need of attention. The appropriation of family time and attention by the drug problem left little available for mundane, yet important, parental tasks like coming to the school play or, watching a child play football, and this was at least noted, if not resented, by siblings:

> It was just sometimes it was just everything about my sister and I was just left aside a bit.
>
> (Sibling: William)

The effects of this imbalanced attention have rarely been noted in research, although some family therapists attentive to these dynamics have noted that younger siblings of addicts are not well integrated with their families. The imbalanced attention to the sibling with the problem means that other siblings tend to be ignored in the face of major family conflicts (Huberty and Huberty 1986). A percipient example of this can be heard in the following mother's reflection on how she had responded to her son's drug problems. She had taken it upon herself to sort the problem and was entirely focused upon him, even at the cost of having her other son move out of the family home:

> R: Yes I kept him [son with drug problem] in the house and my son that stayed with me, Stephen [not using drugs], he wasn't married, he finally walked…he went out the house. I mean I kept saying to him 'well you go because I'll need to stay with him'. He was mine, as if they weren't

both mines (laughs), I mean that was the stage I got to, Sean was mine, the rest could go to hell.

I: How do you mean?

R: Well I didn't want anybody to argue with him, I didn't want anybody to touch him, I didn't want anybody to talk to him, he was mine, I was going to deal with the situation. But I couldn't deal with it.

(Parent: Mrs McNabb)

Similar dynamics have been identified in those families where a child has a chronic health problem that is greatly absorbing of parental attention (Bluebond-Langner 1996). The small amount of research attention on the responses of well siblings to the parental focus on the sick child indicates that even whilst apparently accepting the necessity of the family pulling together, other siblings are often rather guiltily resentful that their own needs for attention are sublimated to the needs of the sick child. This resentment is apparent in the following interview extract. Significantly it is intensified by the contrast between his 'good' behaviour and the undeserving attention received by his brothers.

Just because they're sick or they've got an illness or whatever you want to call it, they seem to get more attention but, I mean, God forbid, this is a horrible thing to say but if they had cancer or something or leukemia, I could totally understand everybody...I mean they'd get all the attention, that's fine, but when they're...they'd steal the sugar out your tea or they'd steal anything that wasn't nailed down and yet they still get welcomed back with open arms.

(Sibling: Martin)

The largely unintended sidelining of other children in the family came about through a sense of parental obligation to help the child in most obvious need. It was however compounded by the sense conveyed by most of the siblings that their family role was at best to be supportive and at worst not to add to the family troubles. The powerful idea of the family as 'all pulling together' in the face of family adversity in a sense justified the siblings' sublimation to the greater need of the brother or sister with the drug problem:

Well I did say to my ma and da that it was really annoying me, but they were saying 'You've just got to stick with us and try and get Andrea through this.'

(Sibling: Andrew)

It seemed from these interviews that there was little scope for the assertion, or resolution, of more individually focused (and less welcome) responses. This was reflected in the interview process itself since it was the rarely the case that parents, or indeed siblings, had considered the broader impacts of having a brother or sister using drugs:

> It was my mum that said to me, when she said that you [researcher: MB] were coming out, she said 'It never even dawned for me to ask you how you felt about it.' And that was six years ago, d'you know what I mean?

> (Sibling: Logan)

A family's response to one of its member's drug problems will inevitably be informed by pre-existing family dynamics. So, for example, one might expect pre-existing sibling rivalries to be played out in a brother or sister's response to, or rationale for, problem drug use. In the interviews with siblings there was a tendency to focus on long-standing perceptions of sibling roles split between 'bad' and 'good' so that comments like 'I always got the blame, I was always the bad yin, I was always the runt of the litter' or 'she's always been the angel' were frequently made by the family member with the drug problem. Rivalries between siblings for their mother's attention and perceived inequities in the distribution of other resources, like money, tended to find focus for expression through the drug problem:

> My boys are good to me, you know and he'll [son with drug problem] say that, 'oh aye your goody goodies'. He'd say 'oh aye…you just think your big sons (laughs) are the whole cheese'.

> (Parent: Mrs McNabb)

The positioning of the sibling with the drug problem as the 'bad' brother or sister meant that other siblings could also conveniently use this for their own ends as a cover for their own transgressions:

> But when she got that wee bit older and started taking the drugs… If something happened I would just blame her and then they would believe me. Which isn't right, d'you know what I mean? I started to play on it a wee bit, I started to use to my advantage. I felt when she buggered off I was left there anyway so I may as well have used it a wee bit to my advantage.

> (Sibling: Logan)

The leverage that this perceived imbalance in parental attention created for the non-drug-using sibling(s) was noted by one of the fathers. The sense of being manipulated added to the discordance:

They [non-drug using sons] got like the addicts with the blackmail stuff. We got so we couldn't say no to them either. I think it was they would see them getting it and then it was 'I'd like to get new £60 football boots' and things, and 'oh we can't afford it' and it was, 'you'd give it to them'. So they got a wee bit wide [savvy] and all, they learned the blackmail trick, 'I'm good, so you should give it to me'.

(Parent: Mr Merrick)

The centre stage occupied by the drug problem in these households was both cause and justification for skewed family dynamics; it was the fuel of family problems and also a resource. In providing a ready-made explanation for any family problem, it justified a cycle of negative reaction that progressively locked the family member with the drug problem into the position of family scapegoat.

The ties that bind and break

These brothers and sisters lamented the loss of the valued role of elder sibling. A 'normal' sibling relationship was supposed to be reciprocally confiding, protective, interested, guiding and supportive, and their relationships looked nothing like this. Of course there is more than an element of wishful thinking in this and anyway, a lack of closeness could be attributable to other things than drugs, were they not so convenient a peg. However, the notion of family was strong in virtually all of the siblings' minds and they did consider that drugs greatly interfered with the kind of relationships they wished they had with their elder brothers or sisters. Siblings described the kinds of relationships they had enjoyed prior to their becoming drug involved, which referred to their relative positions as elder and younger siblings. This is evident in the following, where the younger brother was clearly something of a mascot and his elder sister his protector:

'Em well when I was like five and six she would take me out up to Dennistoun with her pals and that, her friends and just hang about with them... My sister used to spike my hair and stuff like that for me when I was younger.

(Sibling: Andrew)

These siblings wanted elder brothers or sisters they could look up to. Yet through being dishevelled or inebriated or argumentative in public, their elder siblings would reduce, not add, to their social capital:

I used to get people coming up and saying to me 'your sister done this' and 'your sister done that' and pure shouting at me...like [for] stealing off somebody or causing fights or whatever, and I was like 'what do you want me to do?'...I still get it now in fact and I'm like that 'I don't even see the lassie', know what I mean? I don't speak to her.

(Sibling: Marie Louise)

These data also offered a glimpse of the degree to which the conflicts created by an elder sibling's drug related behaviour could expose younger brothers, in particular, to violence:

The closeness just fell away 'cos he just caused trouble for us. Once he went [left the area], we got bullied, first it was my brother Luke and then when he went into the army, it was me. These boys used to wait for us when we came back from school and would give us a doing [beat them], it got to the point that you couldn't even go out to the shops 'cos they'd be waiting for you.

(Sibling: Simon)

It was the distance between their expectations and the reality that siblings emphasized.

And I feel sad because it's as if I don't have a big sister anymore.

(Sibling: Vicki)

The problem was that once drugs came into the picture then everything else assumed secondary importance. Time spent together would fall away as their drug-using sibling was more and more preoccupied with the business of securing and using drugs. Their single-minded focus to the exclusion of everything else distanced them greatly from each other:

He's a hard person to be with...he's very selfish, very...I think when people, anybody, that starts using drugs, they totally lose all reality...they become totally different people...with people that takes drugs it's as if they don't care for life at all, and they don't care about anybody else except for theirselves basically.

(Sibling: Susan)

The expectation that an elder sibling could provide help and advice was seldom realized. Younger siblings felt they could not turn to elder siblings with their troubles both out of a sense of their greater relative problems and because they felt they were just not interested anyway:

Just wish she would be like...just be like a normal sister, an older sister. I'd like to have been able to go to her with problems but I can't do it for some reason, I don't know how…I think it's because really that Andrea has got problems with the drugs and that and I don't want to hit her with other problems when she's got problems of her own.

(Sibling: Andrew)

Their disinclination to turn to their brothers or sisters was reinforced by their difficulties in communicating or even maintaining any interest when intoxicated:

Or even just sitting watching him when he's wrecked, you're like 'shut up' 'cos he just talks rubbish. He talks a lot of rubbish and it's 'feel sorry for me'. … And it's quite frustrating, that's what frustrates me more. See actually just seeing him totally, like totally gone with it, when he's that way he can hardly speak. One minute he's speaking to you, the next minute he's…what is it they call it, ducking for apples.

(Sibling: Martina)

Rather than aligning themselves with their siblings, these interviews suggested the greater likelihood that siblings would distance themselves from them and take on defensive roles to protect their mothers whom they saw as unfairly burdened by their elder brother's or sister's problems. These siblings were regularly entering into the fray, often to defend the mother from some of the onslaughts from the drug-using sibling. The following mother describes just one such scenario:

She knows that he's selfish; she knows the hassle that he's causing me, and she doesn't like that. She's more mad at that fact. Because we had a couple of episodes as I say when me and him were right into it…I mean we were nose to nose and I was screaming at him to get out the house…and the abuse I was getting, and twice, she was nose to nose to him, she came out the room, she actually pushed me out the road and she was nose to nose with him – 'don't you talk to my mother like that', you know, 'who the hell do you think you are?' and…she was standing there and she wasn't going to move. You would need to bulldoze through her, you know what I mean sort of a thing.

(Parent: Mrs Smith)

One effect was that these siblings could become over-involved in the family conflict and by acting as their mother's protectors, created cross-generational alliances that intensified problems between siblings and possibly, too, between parents.

Many recovering drug users have spoken of how their efforts to rebuild their lives were often motivated by a desire to get back to the person they were before drugs intervened in their lives (McIntosh and McKeganey 2001). This 'essential self' untainted by drugs was remembered by parents and brothers and sisters and contrasted with the way in which they had been diminished by drugs:

> Oh I know the person that's using the drugs is not the son I had, I understand that, that's a shell of the person I knew...I mean all I see is an addict, I don't see my son anymore because I know that's not my son, definitely isn't my son.
>
> (Parent: Mr Bell)

During periods of recovery, the family reported feeling that their relative had been returned to them again:

> I: Right. And do you sort of think there's a difference between the person she is when she's using drugs and the person when she's not using drugs?
>
> R: Definitely because when she's on drugs, she just doesn't care about you, she just doesn't want to know, she's just interested in herself but the real person, she's nice and she's funny and she's caring and stuff.
>
> (Sibling: Danielle)

However, over time, the chronic cycles of relapse and recovery that characterize most drug careers chipped away at the hope for a relationship unfettered by the baggage of the drug problem. The hope that, this time, their son or daughter, sister of brother would become free of drugs was harder to maintain after numerous episodes in treatment and subsequent relapse. Over time it appeared to become harder to hold onto this memory of what their child or sibling had been and sadly, too, there appeared to be a leaking away of faith that this return journey could be made:

> I hope for the same as any parent hopes for; that my boys'll get out this shite and get a bit a life and...you know, make a wee home for themselves and get a bit a future and maybe have a family or whatever, know, but... I've learned not to expect anything, know, I think that's maybe the saddest thing about it – that I don't expect anything... I'd be very surprised if any of my boys get through this, know, the two that's using. I think the best I can hope for is burying them, I don't think...you know, I think that's the last thing I'll get to do for them, I don't think they'll get through this, you know, I think it's been too long now.
>
> (Parent: Mr Merrick)

This father's bleak assessment of the situation was based on his two son's drug careers of over ten years and their subsequent development of mental health problems. This pessimism, grounded in an unfathomable sadness, was shared by very many of the parents in this study. The siblings were, on the whole, slightly more hopeful, although they too could see a time when this fund of faith might run out, if their brother or sister could not find a way out of drug dependence. The following brother felt he had reached a point of no return in his relationship with his brother:

> Me and Sam will never ever be close again, we talk you know we're civil to each other now, but you can see it; there is no bond there. I would never ever want anything bad to happen to him you know, but at the same time I really wouldn't be surprised if something did…There isn't very much love between me and Nick now and there's certainly no trust.
>
> (Sibling: David)

Conclusion

The effort to cope with a family member's severe and chronic drug problem appears to create a gross distortion of family roles. Rather like the cuckoo in the nest, the drug problem comes to achieve a dominant position within the family dynamic, closely intervening in every aspect of family life. The severe stress that families experience in the lurch from crisis to crisis both causes and contributes to the fractured family response to the drug problem. Relations between parents, and between parents and children, appear all to be bent out of shape by the effects of living with the drug problem and the lack of agreement on how best to respond to it. And this often goes on for as many years as their child or brother or sister has a drug problem, perhaps without any end in sight.

In the face of this long term and chronic situation it ought to be both surprising and shocking that there has been so little in the way of co-ordinated response to families living with the drug problem of their son or daughter, brother or sister. It is to this matter that the following chapter on the responses of a small number of practitioners to the problem turns.

Chapter 4

Practitioner Responses to Mothers and Fathers, Brothers and Sisters of Problem Drug Users

Introduction

Living with the problems brought about by drugs creates recurrent, often acute, stresses for families. On the whole though they struggle through these alone. Their social isolation is compounded by the lack of institutional recognition of the burdens on these families and the costs to their social, physical and mental wellbeing.

This chapter considers the perceptions of a small number of practitioners (10) involved either directly with problem drug users in their practice or indirectly through teaching children with brothers or sisters who have drug problems. These practitioners comprised drug workers, teachers, child and family social workers and general practitioners, as well as voluntary sector family support workers. One would, of course, be right to hesitate in setting too much store by so small a sample. Nonetheless, the commonality of themes identified across the sample and their mesh with the reported experiences of families provides a good rationale for their identification and discussion here.

A first key point is that the client group framed the focus of the practitioners. In these interviews with practitioners the teachers were concerned with the children to be educated; drug workers with the adult with the drug problem (and in the case of the agency employing these particular drug workers, their children too). Predictably, children were the focus of interest for child and family social workers. The nature of the work of the general practitioner (GP) made for a broader vision, although here too, the gaze was more focused where young children were concerned. The rather atomized focus of services unsurprisingly often meant that the bigger picture of how drug problems differentially affect family members and families became lost. The, perhaps obvious, exception to this tendency to see the drug problem in its constituent parts and according to a hierarchy of need or vulnerability, rather than in the round, were the family support workers. Their personal experiences of the impacts that the drug problem had on their own families were the essential starting point for their perception of the whole family as drug affected.

The family as a resource

Where the client (the problem drug user, the child) is the focal point of concern, there are obvious conceptual difficulties in also seeing things from the perspectives of other family members. The drug and social workers and, to a lesser extent, the GPs, were inclined to see the extended family as a potential *resource* providing a supportive family infrastructure for the person with the drug problem or their children. One can see an example of this in the following interview extract where a drug worker's understanding of the place of family was framed by her sense of the needs of the mothers and children in the residential drug unit she worked in:

> We would try to encourage all these relationships because we think that the mothers would need as much help as they can get when they are outside [leave the rehabilitation unit], especially from family, because family will take the children and the children feel safe.

> (Drugs worker 1)

The effects upon the family in being supportive were not necessarily part of this reckoning. On the whole, consideration of these was largely focused on balancing the benefits of the family support *for* the client, against the possibility that the family input might have a destabilizing effect on the client. Practitioners are trained to prepare care plans that are client centred and about 'prioritizing what the problems are' (GP1), identifying 'who in the family is the positive support' (social worker). Working from a client-centric perspective, the family is assessed in terms of its role as supportive or otherwise. Whilst appreciating the disturbance and anguish experienced by families trying to cope with a family member's drug problem, the practitioners' inevitable focus on problem solving from the point of view of their client meant that they were less well equipped to alleviate this distress.

The voluntary family support groups had a different take on the matter, which was predictable given that they usually had personal experience of the impact of problem drug use on their own families. They began from the premise that they were dealing with a family problem:

It's a family illness, not just the person with the illness…and it changes everyone. It's a very devastating thing to come through.

(Family support worker 1)

As parents of children with drug problems, it was they who provided that support, often over many years. It was in recognition of the many costs to the family of providing this support that these family support groups were set up. They had an explicit remit to support the family, and this might mean helping parents and siblings into *not* continuing to support the child with the drug problem. From the perspective of the family support groups, it was important to stress the limits to that support:

We ask them [parents], what's changed? See all the stuff you've been doing? Has it changed them? I say 'well what have you got to do? You need to change; you need to change the way you deal with them and the way you deal with the rest of the family. The stuff you've been doing, it's not working'… We've got a saying here 'saying no helps, saying yes hurts'. The more you say yes to the addict; the more life will hurt you.

(Family support worker 2)

As family doctors, GPs are better placed to consider family problems in the round. One doctor in particular could draw on a deep well of community knowledge through long years of working in the same practice. Through his clinical practice with members of drug-affected families he appreciated the long-term costs to families and the complexities of family dynamics. It was this experience that allowed him the confidence to intervene where he judged it safe and helpful to do so and it was this that marked him off from most of the other practitioners, including the other GP interviewed. He saw his role as helping the rest of the family to come to terms with the drug problem and 'to allow them to develop the necessary skills to deal with it in the family' (GP2).

All GPs have a duty of confidence to their individual patients, which necessarily prevents sharing information between family members and underscores the sensitivity required to intervene. As the GP noted, this presented tricky terrain but through treading carefully and with due respect he felt able to try to address the issue with all the affected parties:

Most often I do this interview with the drug user's consent. I've actually said in no uncertain terms [to the parent of the drug user] 'if certain things happen then it's your duty to abandon'… So that very often one has had situations which are clearly bad for everyone, the drug user included, because of the continued support or rescue of the drug user in situations which they should never have been rescued from. To some extent there's a double role there; saying 'look you've got to let go but that doesn't mean there aren't other resources, the person has got to individually make up their own mind to use those resources'. That's the challenging part from my point of view, to judge that correctly.

(GP2)

The least likely family member to attract the attention of service providers, or indeed the family support groups, was the brother or sister of the problem drug user. The apparent tendency for siblings to be sidelined by the unfolding family tragedy seems to also play out in service provision, very possibly due to the hierarchical ordering of need and vulnerability. The vulnerability of siblings might have been less obvious because it tended to be mediated by the parent(s); nonetheless, living with high levels of stress and calamity, as well as their proximity to drugs carried significant costs to them too. The service focus of both social workers and drug workers meant that they could not really conceptualize the sibling in terms other than the help they might, or might not, offer to their client group. However, as we saw in Chapters 2 and 3, siblings are greatly affected by the drug-related problems of their brother or sister. Furthermore, as we shall see in Chapter 8, siblings of problem drug users are at elevated risk of developing drug problems themselves.

The perception of siblings as somewhat peripheral can be heard in the following extract in which the possible effects on the sibling are ranked as 'not really relevant' (GP1), unlike those of parents of problem drug users or children of parents with drug problems:

They are not really my most major immediate concern...because siblings are not always that close are they and there's conflict there perhaps...[siblings] just have to learn to adapt and live with it, not let it dominate your life, survival or something.

(GP1)

The impact on siblings' health and mental welfare, because apparently less acute, was less worthy of attention. Other practitioners were more likely to take account of the compounding distress for siblings but again this was largely framed in terms of decision-making as to the potential use of the sibling as a resource to assist the needs of their client:

I: What are the main issues for families?

SW: The stresses and strains it can put on family members. The worries of being unsure as to what is going to happen with them, how safe it is for them… And for families it's about what help they can give as a family member, which is very significant and different from the help they get from support agencies.

(Social worker 1)

For teachers the issues were necessarily differently framed; their concern was with the child to be educated, whatever their background. Whilst placing great emphasis on their primary role to educate, these head teachers recognized and made allowances for children coming from difficult or disturbed backgrounds:

Generally all of the staff in here as far as possible, if we are aware that there's a problem with drugs in the home, that we are a bit more considerate.

(Head teacher 2)

Teachers recognized that their pupils were affected by family problems but on the whole were keen to encourage children to leave these at the door, to see school as a haven from these problems and a place where each pupil could find succour in a community of their peers:

I think that quite often they want to forget about it, they want to find out about the Romans, they want to go to PE [physical education] and sometimes they don't want to think about all the hassle they have at home, because it's like six hours of escape in here and they get the opportunity to be children.

(Head teacher 1)

These primary schoolteachers emphasized the limits to their involvement in the family through focusing on the individual child to be educated. Importantly too, they saw themselves as working in partnership with parents with the expectation that families were in the driver's seat:

I don't think the school can be the answer to everybody's problems and I do think even though you want to help people, there are people who really don't want to be helped and there are people you can't help because you don't have the expertise or the resources. You do the best you can but I do think the best thing is to build up a rapport with the parent or the guardian, say 'we're here, the common denominator here is the child, we're trying to do our best for your child, we know that you're trying to do your best for your child, this is what we can do to help you tackle it'… In the end I am here to educate the child.

(Head teacher 1)

This close definition of the client and service remit was true of virtually all of the practitioners interviewed. This segmentation was not an apparently intentional outcome, but a product of a prevalent model of service delivery that in being highly individualized tends to miss the influential interplay of family relationships and roles and their effect on all family members' behaviours. It is just possible that a more family-centred approach that takes into account these dynamics, and works with them as they play out between family members, could achieve some alleviation of the near intolerable stresses that families seem to experience. This kind of family systems therapeutic work is not common. It is difficult, resource-intensive work and undoubtedly requires very skilful management given the emotional tenor of such intervention. As many of these practitioners described, intervention with families, even in the limited terms of enlisting help for their client, invited great caution.

Reluctance to involve family members

All of the practitioners referred to the complex and very often turbulent family histories that many of their clients reported. Their wariness over involving other members of the family stemmed from a sense of the complexity of these dynamics and the possibility that intervention might do more harm than good, given their inevitably imperfect grasp of the full family dynamic:

> Because the help they [family member] can offer will always be complicated by the kinds of emotions of it, which is different from agencies where the emotional support is there but you are not emotionally tied to them as a person…that takes its toll on the family member.
>
> (Social worker 2)

Difficult family histories invited caution on the part of practitioners in considering whether or not to involve other family members. This can be seen in this GP's balancing of whether or not it would be right to involve siblings:

> There's the usual thing between brothers and sisters etc. of the rivalries and the histories of things that have gone before. There's so many dynamics, from siblings who have always been very dominant so that the drug user has always been dominated by this and therefore is this the right thing to try and resuscitate? That dominant bit can go to full abuse. I mean we've got families where the elder sibs have abused physically and sexually – or both – their own siblings as children. So, one has to be

pretty careful about siblings, because it may not be the best thing to resuscitate something that is better left as history.

(GP 2)

Practitioners were justifiably wary of exacerbating problems for siblings, of exposing them to the full force of their brother or sister's drug problem and of burning them out through involving them too nearly in the problem:

And I think as well, like any brother–sister, sister–sister relationship, there's tension there, natural tension there that would be probably be there whether there was drug or alcohol use anyway. I think some of that can get magnified to make it difficult for both of the individuals. I think looking at some of the issues for individuals who are involved in drug or alcohol abuse and feeling very, very guilty for the stress that they're giving their brother and sisters and feeling very grateful for the help they are getting but also feel concerned that they are not going to live up to the expectations of their brothers and sisters.

(Drug worker 2)

This drug worker identified a volatile cocktail of emotions: guilt, expectation, obligation, pre-existing relational difficulties, each of which could potentially derail any effort on the part of the practitioner to use the resources of one sibling to help the other.

Another reason why practitioners did not include the extended family in the treatment and care of their problem drug-using clients was on account of the client's stated reluctance to involve them. The following drug worker said that as an agency they took their lead from this, although clearly with some reservations:

What we have found in the past, maybe one of the reasons we haven't worked with the extended family, is that many women are estranged from their families, maybe just dumped them, got fed up with them, have stolen from them, had arguments from them, fallen out with them, attacked, assaulted them, charged them, all these various kinds of things. But I think if we could involve them, I think the extended family is what the children need and I think it's what the mothers need.

(Drug worker 1)

The sense that seeking to involve the wider family might be akin to opening a Pandora's box was a source of concern for these professionals, which could serve to justify a narrow focus on the person with drug problem and, depending on the agency, their children. However, it was also clear from their accounts that they could see the merits of a broader therapeutic involvement, which incorporated working with the problem from multiple perspectives. The account of the drug worker above, in listing the drug-associated damage to relationships, also indicated the potential for such remedial work where the problem drug user is trying to put their drug use behind them. Indeed it is hard to argue with the notion that it is precisely at this time that the work of building bridges between family members could most usefully occur. Alleviating social isolation and the associated social stress through initiating the work of repairing family relationships and building a reliable social network could be crucially important in sustaining recovery from drugs.

Conclusion

Currently most services to problem drug users and their families are need driven; children need education and protection, drug users need treatment and everyone needs health care. These remits inevitably structure practitioners' understanding of, and response to, clients. By and large this is an individual affair, focused on aspects of a person's needs or behaviour rather than the whole. Framed in terms of meeting individual needs it is easy to see how a practitioner might focus more on the usefulness of the family to meeting the needs of the client than on the effects this has on the family. Testimony to this is the lack of attention paid to parents of problem drug users and even more starkly the brothers and sisters of siblings with drug problems. Where need is so individually structured, the needs of others can easily become institutionally invisible.

This institutional tendency to dissect the problem through the prioritization of individual need also represents something of a missed opportunity to find therapeutic means by which families can be helped to recognize and utilize their own considerable resources to support each other, to have some insight into their family calamity and to arrest the chain of negative reaction set in place by the problem drug use of one of their members. An alternative model therefore might be to suggest working with family dynamics, rather than in spite of them. I shall return to this issue in the final chapter, which discusses in more detail some of the emergent implications for policy and practice in working with families.

From here however, the book shifts tack, to look at what happens when the person with the drug problem becomes a parent and the consequences of this for their families and, most significantly, their children.

Chapter 5

Parenting in the Midst of a Drug Problem

Introduction

Drug dependence imposes exacting rhythms around the financing and securing of drugs that can wholly preoccupy the daily round. Children rarely fit neatly into these activities both because the illegality and costs associated with drugs add an inevitable unpredictability to the process of their procurement and use and because children have their own equally exacting needs. The push and pull between the needs imposed by drugs and by children form the focus of this chapter. As we shall see, the capacity for problem drug use to be experienced by parents as overwhelming can result in very vulnerable children.

This chapter looks at the ways in which parents talked about trying to manage their drug problem whilst also being responsible for the care of their children. Out of the 62 parents interviewed in the study on parents and children ('Growing up in drug dependent households', Barnard *et al.* 2000): a third were drug free, a third were using prescribed methadone and a third were engaged in chaotic or uncontrolled drug use at the time of interview. Sampling in this way had the advantage of being able to compare between stages of drug use and their relative impact on parenting. Those parents who were now drug free reflected on the relationship between their drug problem and parenting capacities and compared this with their current sense of themselves as parents.

Efforts were made to recruit men who were the main carers. However, the great majority of those interviewed were mothers, as they were almost always the parent with the main childcare responsibility. A high proportion of women were parenting alone (64%). Current relationships among problem drug-using women were, with one exception, with men who also had drug problems. As reported in other research (Chance and Scannapieco 2002), these relationships were not characterized by permanency and only in an absolute minority of cases were the mother and father of the same child or children both resident in the same household. Typically these were households headed by single women but which were shared for periods of time with others, including boyfriends who might take on a fathering role of any resident children during the time they lived in the same household.

Premise

In this area one often hears the statement that problem drug use does not necessarily mean an inability to parent a child. This chapter will argue that it is only under conditions of stringent and controlled drug use (whether methadone or illegal) that children are not negatively affected by their parent's drug problem. Inevitably this is an argument that treads rocky moral terrain that is uncomfortably close to victimization of an already socially excluded and stigmatized section of the population (Barnard 2005a). Labelling reduces people, and so diminishes the complex histories that have led to problem drug use. Many of these parents might be characterized as victims themselves, given their frequent accounts of childhoods marred by abuse and family dysfunction, for which they carried the scars, even if their family situation had since altered. However, there is a distinction to be made between the person with the drug problem and the effects that their drug-associated behaviours have on others, particularly dependent children. This is not a chapter about demonizing parents; it is about recognizing the power of drug problems to overwhelm just about everything else in that person's life. The distinction is nicely drawn in the excerpt below:

> Good and evil are names for what people do, not what they are. All we can say is that this a good deed because it helps someone, or that is a bad deed because it hurts them. People are too complicated to have simple labels.
>
> (*The Amber Spyglass*, Pullman 2000, p.471)

Drawing on the interviews with parents I will first outline their views on the force of their dependency problems and then move to depict some of the routines associated with drug use as a means of showing how these necessarily impinge upon the care and wellbeing of children, even despite the efforts of the parent to protect them from exposure to drugs and the associated lifestyle.

The compulsion of drugs

A constant theme throughout the interviews with parents was the compelling force of drugs in their lives once they had become dependent upon them. It was described variously as 'taking everything away from them' as 'driving them', as making them selfish and self-absorbed. Preoccupation with getting and using drugs was described almost universally and can be seen in the following interview extract:

> If you're taking the heroin, that's your master, know...I don't know anybody that's been able to do it yet; take the drug and look after their family and things like that...that's the bottom line, it just doesn't work, I've never known it to work anyway. I've seen it all over the years and I don't think there's anybody that's managed it.
>
> (Parent: Frank)

The salient question is not really one of whether or not these parents loved their children, it is more one of their ability to meet their children's needs, to care for them and keep them safe whilst so preoccupied with their drug use. Most parents felt trapped within their compulsion for drugs and the drive to use them; even in the face of all the dangers that such use entailed, the costs to themselves and to their children:

> It's not bad people that become addicts and it's not bad people that don't care about their kids, it's just people that an addiction has got a grip of and that that is more powerful than anything, even the love that a parent would have for their children, it just overrules even that.
>
> (Parent: Alexa)

A stark indication of the primary place drugs came to occupy in their lives lay in the commonly made statement that if it came to a choice between getting and using the drugs and attending to the children, it would almost always be the drug use that would win out.

> Because we never bothered with him [their son], drugs always came first, it didn't matter what was wrong with him, drugs always came first.
>
> (Parents: Hamish and Anna)

One parent now recovering from her drug problems described in harsh terms how her preoccupation with drugs made her selfish:

> 'Cos you only care about yourself, you think you care about everybody else but number one comes first and that's yourself and if you're lucky, if you've got anything left, they get it, but you would take it off them to

give to you and anybody that says...I mean at the time I wouldn't admit that, but now I would...

(Parent: Jocelyn)

The woman in the following interview extract acknowledged just how frequently she faces this moment when she knows she can spend the money one of two ways. As is clear from her narrative she is clear how she *should* spend it, but each time comes to a different decision:

I stand with a tenner (£10) in my hand and I think...'What will I do? Will I give they weans money to spend, or will I go and buy this? Or will I go and buy a bag [of heroin]?' And it always seems to come down to buying a bag.

(Parent: Mary)

Mary had the good fortune to be able to rely on her mother to step into the breach and this undoubtedly would have been a factor tipping the balance. However, there were those parents who did not have the option to rely on family members and who would come to similar conclusions. It was not that there was no inclination to find what was necessary to the children, like food or nappies, the important thing was to remove uncertainty over the provision of drugs. Once money for drugs was secured they could start to attend to the business of securing the children's needs, but in that order.

I mean you had a fiver or a tenner in that hand and you're like that, 'well I've got nothing for my dinner the night, but I've not got any drugs either'. You'd go and buy the drugs and then say 'och I'll ask my neighbour for something for dinner' or I'll go over and see my ma, make up to my ma the excuse that my freezer broke down and all my food's all melted, 'going to give us something for my dinner' or, 'my giro [social security payment] never came or something'... just to tide you over 'til the next day when you would tap [borrow from] somebody else or...

(Parent: Julia)

Such assertions can be quite difficult to hear as they so categorically elevate a fixation with drug use over meeting the needs of children. These parents considered that an essential feature of their problem with drugs was that it overwhelmed everything else, particularly if that use was uncontrolled.

The physiological and psychological sense of dependence described by these parents meant making choices that compromised their abilities to parent their children safely. Those parents who were now in recovery from drugs spoke of a mindset narrowly focused on immediate concerns with getting and using drugs and an accompanying rationale that justified the elevation of their drug needs: that without them they could not function and could not care for the children:

> Y'know it's all about denial and justification…and the unacceptable becoming the acceptable. I think they three things are the main things that are in your life, you're justifying everything, you're denying how bad it is and you're doing things that you wouldn't normally do or you're letting things happen that you would never normally let happen.
>
> (Parent: Mhairi)

In the middle of drug dependency problems, this narrow focus on drugs is probably what sustains the determination to find and use drugs, often against quite remarkable odds. It is also what makes their children most vulnerable because it armours parents against seeing the damage they can do to their children:

> See as long as your wean's got something to eat, you think that's the thing, whether it be a Mars Bar or cereal or something, like, 'they're all right'. In your head you know that's not right, but then again you're like, 'they're getting something to eat anyway, they'll be fine'. As long as they're quiet, they're all right. Just give them something – 'here play with that', to carry on whatever I'm doing. Likesay if I'm having a hit or something, or whatever. 'Just play with that, do that, wreck the place', as long as they're quiet.
>
> (Parent: Mel)

Drug stability

Those parents whose drug use was stable were better able to focus on their children and other aspects of their lives once freed from the stresses associated with funding and maintaining an illegal drug habit. Usually this meant a stable daily dose of methadone, although not exclusively, as one woman reported a highly routinized pattern of injected use of non-prescribed Buprenorphine over many years. The following woman contrasted her current positive situation with her child with what it had been like to parent when she was dependent upon illegal drugs:

> Then, it was just I fed him, changed him, got him what he needed, d'you know what I mean, we didn't have a relationship, 'em…now I know what he likes and I know what he doesn't like, I take an interest in what he does, 'em, everything's so different, so, so different now…just everything…it's funny you don't really realize they're there, d'you know

what I mean, as I say, it's just feed him, change him, give him money for the van and this and that and the next thing, but just to see him doing things, see what makes him happy, what doesn't make him happy, all different things, it's just so different.

(Parent: Ariana)

The ability to institute and follow routines based around their children was the biggest single difference that these women noted once they had come into calmer waters and were using a stable dose of methadone and nothing else:

His life's totally changed, it's totally turned around because now he gets his breakfast made for him whereas before that didn't happen. When he comes home from school I'm there, his washing is done, dried, put away; his bedroom's kept spotless clean, whereas none of that happened [before]. He's got the best of clothes, he's got the same as all the other boys have, like when I was still on it he didn't have, it was all the cheap stuff that ye bought. He goes places, me and him joined the Sports Centre together, we go there, know, we go to the swimming and things.

(Parent: Hailey)

However, being maintained on a methadone prescription is not the same thing as being stable on that prescription. This is an important distinction. In these data, a minority of parents (n=6 of 21 parents sampled from methadone clinics) considered themselves stable on methadone. The rest were using illegal drugs on top of their prescribed methadone doses, often quite substantially. The great majority of the parents interviewed all testified to the enormous hold that drugs still had on every aspect of their lives.

There is a certain drama in asserting that drugs can come to exert such power over a person but it is an essential element in understanding something of the processes by which children can come to assume a secondary place to drugs and in the process become vulnerable to harm. This next section looks at the way in which a drug problem can come to dominate the whole structure of the day and how this in turn leaves little time or energy available to see to the needs of their children, whether on an emotional, physical or social level.

The daily round

Probably the only routine they had was my drug use and me getting my drugs, that was the only routine.

(Parent: Alexa)

Drug dependency imposes exacting but fundamentally unpredictable routines. The business of funding, locating and using drugs described by these parents was frequently arduous and uncertain. Where money might be available for drugs one day, the next it might not; where drugs might today be obtained from a nearby source, the next day that dealer might have disappeared, entailing an uncertain chase around the city to locate another source. The illegality and costs of drugs make their supply and access inevitably unpredictable. A certain relentlessness was apparent in the interviews, as success in getting and using drugs would, in a relatively short space of time, lead to the effects wearing off and the need to fund, find and buy more would be reasserted. This repeating cycle of the search for money and drugs carried on through the day, and often the night too, irrespective of mealtimes, the school day, bad weather and good.

To illustrate something of the difficulty of grafting childcare routines onto the rhythms that drug dependence imposes it is worth considering some concrete examples. Start with the beginning of the day. Mornings were difficult times for many of the parents:

> They [children] knew the days we had money and the days we didn't have money, we'd get up and we'd be rattling and the only thing you'd be thinking about is 'how can I get money to get squared up and then get the weans to school' and things like that, know what I mean, because you couldn't be annoyed getting their clothes out, getting them all ironed, getting them all ready unless you were feeling alright yourself, know what I mean…like a Monday it was always a bad day for money and most Mondays they would've been off school, know what I mean, because I would've been pure ill…they were off quite a lot.
>
> (Parent: Rona)

A few parents spoke of saving enough drugs for use in the morning, but many more described the difficulties of saving drugs for later. The more likely scenario was that they would use the drugs until they were finished and only then sleep:

> While I was going up the town [working as a prostitute], I was taking punters back to the flat. While he [partner] was in the living room with the wean, I was just straight into the [bed] room and then as soon as I was done I was going and scoring and sometimes trying to keep a bit by for the next morning but you just couldn't do it, keep a bit by for the next morning 'cause it's sitting there, staring at you right in the face so I ended up taking it and then the morning comes and you're rattling [withdrawing] and I'm like that, 'I'm not even going to change her

nappy until I get a charge – she can wait' and it's just not right but you don't think of things like that until you come into a place like this [residential detox facility].

(Parent: Angela)

On waking, children need to be changed from their nightclothes, have their breakfasts and get to school and nursery on time. Each of these was greatly affected by the drug problem.

I couldn't look after Sarah when I was strung out, I had to have drugs in me. I'd be shouting and bawling at her and a couple of times I even sort of a hit her, know I was violent. I wouldn't get her dressed or anything until I had my drugs in me, but it was a real struggle, you know to get up off the chair ... so she was left to her own devices sort of a, you know, wander about the house with just underwear on, or her nightie, from the night before.

(Parent: Hilary)

The following mother describes how it would be in the morning on waking without drugs available. In her need and haste to get them, she would regularly put her baby into the pram and go in search of drugs without feeding or changing him.

When Kevin [partner] was there, it was Kevin would go, and if we had money or whatever, go and get money and go and get the drugs. But when Kevin went into rehab, the first thing I would do in the morning, I wouldn't even get Jacob changed or feed him, it would be straight up, into the pram and go and...maybe if I'd to go to the Post Office or something first or whatever and Jacob would get fed and changed after that.

(Parent: Grace)

Young children and babies are the most vulnerable because they are the most dependent on their caregivers. The risks that the following mother reported clearly show this vulnerability where drugs are accorded greater priority than children:

I want to be able to...just be like a normal young mother and be able to get up in the morning, get her ready first thing in the morning, take her up the park and feed the ducks and all that with her instead of getting up and thinking 'oh no, where am I going to get my next hit from before I can change her or do anything like that?' Know, it was just when I was rattling and all that that, I was like that; 'I don't want her near me, just keep her away from me, I can't cope with her' or he'd [partner] say 'are you going to change her?' And I'd be like that; 'och I'll get her in a minute, I'll get her in a minute, I'll make her something in a minute' and it would always be a minute, a minute, a minute and sometimes she even went a day without even getting anything to eat, it was just like bottles I was giving her, filling it with milk and saying 'there you go'.

(Parent: Angela)

Children were reportedly very frequently late or absent from school because of the difficulties many parents experienced in establishing routinized bedtimes and getting up in the morning. This might be especially the case where women use prostitution as a means of income. This is not uncommon in Glasgow, which has a large street working population that is dominated by women with drug problems (McKeganey and Barnard 2002). Working into the small hours would often mean sleeping through the earlier part of the day. To achieve this might require trying to engineer a situation where the child's routines were calibrated with those imposed by the drug use. As can be heard this was stressful for all concerned but, equally clearly, it was not a situation that took any account of the child's best interests:

I: And what was it like in terms of routines and all that sort of stuff with Charlie [toddler]?

R: Well I mean there wasn't any, you would try to keep him up late so he would sleep, or I would say to Dave [dad] 'keep him [son] up late 'cause I'm coming in late and I want to sleep during the day' and things like this and if I came back maybe eight or nine at night for a hit, he would have the light off and be trying to force Charlie to go to sleep and I used to shout and bawl, 'you go out and get the fucking money and I'll watch him 'cause I would do a better job than you', you know it was a shame and I'm like that, 'get the fucking light on and let him play with the toys, he's not ready to go to sleep ...' you know it was a shame.

(Parent: Taylor)

Also, because drugs were so preoccupying, there were those parents who spoke of wanting an easy life. If their child did not want to go to school they were not going to spend a lot of time fighting with them over it:

I wasn't putting them into school, they didn't want to go to school – that was fair enough, 'och just stay off school, it's alright'. I wasn't putting them out to school, they were just running a savvy [wild] and 'em I was always getting complaints, 'your sons are doing this', 'your sons are doing that', 'your sons are doing this'. They were wild.

(Parent: Nicky)

This was not true of all parents. There were those who saw the benefits of school to protect their children from over-exposure to their drug use and they encouraged attendance on that basis:

I always remember thinking like she's got to get to school, she's got to get to school because I knew she'd get her dinner there and she'd be away, she wouldn't really see anything during the day. I was sort of a...even though I was stoned, I had that in the back of my mind, 'I don't want her to see anything so she's better off at school' and probably, eh, I knew that I would get into trouble and all that if she wasn't at school so I sort of always made sure that she got to school.

(Parents: Hilary)

Wrapped up in this too was the opportunity to meet her drug needs unimpeded by her child and this was also a spur to ensuring regular school or nursery attendance:

I really tried to make sure that she got to nursery because I had to go out and do other things and I didn't want this wean with me, she was a burden.

(Parent: Hilary)

Parents on a methadone prescription would also face some stress in the morning as getting to the pharmacy for the daily dose of methadone would be constrained by opening times and, in the meantime, children still had to be attended to.

Difficult choices

Even considering this very small window into the day, one can see the conflict that sets up between meeting the needs of the child and those of the parent's drug problem. Considered in terms of the day's routines it is clear that things do not get any easier, with these same tensions being played out all through the day. The following parent, for example, describes a dilemma often encountered at the end of her son's school day:

Say I went out, you know, during the day and you'd every intention to be back in time for him coming in from school, now he was only five and six, right, now some nights I wasn't getting back 'til six o'clock so that wean was coming home from school, nobody in, so he was putting his wee school bag and things underneath the hedge and going away and playing about the streets until I came home. And it was a case of I'd be away looking for my fix and couldn't go home until I'd got that, knowing fine well that that wean was up the road playing about, waiting on me coming back.

(Parent: Hailey)

During the hours that this young child waited for his mother to arrive home, he was without shelter if it rained, and he was in the dark if it was winter. He was alone, unsupervised and, more to the point, nobody knew he was there. As his mother also commented, anything could have happened to him.

Where children were not in school or nursery, parents were faced each time with the choice to take children with them to locate and buy drugs or, to leave them. Both of these scenarios are problematic in so far as the child is concerned. One can hear something of the mental gymnastics that a parent might have to perform to square her need to obtain drugs with what this would entail for her children and their safety:

I used to take my kids…I always used to say these people that leave their kids in the house on their own, they're the bad parents. But I used to be a good parent 'cos I used to take my kids with me to score and we'd stand out in the rain for three hours waiting on somebody coming back with drugs but I was still a good parent 'cos I had my children standing beside me, it didn't matter that it was 11 o'clock at night and they were soaking and they were hungry and they were tired and I think that's all the lies that you've got to lie to yourself to be able to get through life with.

(Parent: Alexa)

If the parent takes the child there is the possibility of their exposure to criminality, to other drug users, to seeing drug use, including drug injection. If, as a means of reducing the likelihood of exposure to the actual drug transactions, the parent makes the choice to leave children outside the house, they may well be unsupervised and so exposed to other danger. This may be particularly the case if the parent decides to take the drugs on the premises, thus expanding the time that children are left outside.

Of course, there is no guarantee that drugs will be readily available and many of these parents spoke of long treks around the city to find them, going in taxis if there was enough money, or on buses and on foot if there was not. One gets a sense of the tedium and discomfort of being hostage to the vagaries of supply from the following account:

'Cos a few times like, before I started dealing myself, I used to have to take him with me to go and buy and that's one thing I hated, d'you know what I mean, dragging the wean with you. Into these houses that nobody knows and they're all lying about full of it and you're like that 'phew...' but he [son] must've known, know what I mean, and then I've took him half way along Easterhouse and down to Carntyne and trekking away up here. You'd walk for miles. Just to get something. If this person didn't have it, you'd walk to Easterhouse, if they didn't have it, you'd walk to the other side of Easterhouse. If they didn't have it, you'd go to Cranhill. I've actually walked nearly the whole of Glasgow.

(Parent: Julia)

What then if the child is not taken to buy drugs? The obvious concern in this case is one of supervision. There were instances where children were reportedly left with friends, or with grandparents and other relatives, when going to buy drugs. Given the repeating cycle of funding, locating and using drugs on an everyday basis, and often more than once a day, there is an obvious precariousness to arrangements that relied on the extended good will and availability of friends. Of course there is the possibility that the friend might also be using drugs, as a feature of drug careers over time is the distance from association with non-drug-using friends (McIntosh and McKeganey 2001). There were children who had been left with 'friends' who hurt them physically and, in two other cases, had sexually abused them, underlining the point that where drugs are the most preoccupying concern the suitability of the carer might be a lesser priority.

Such arrangements had greater stability where the extended family was involved, as they were often all too aware of the potential costs to the children and wanted to protect them from possible harm. As we shall see in Chapter 7 the role of the extended family in taking responsibility to care for children was often critical in protecting them from harm and preventing their removal into care. However there were other instances in these data where parents did not have the option to call on others and had made the decision to leave the child unsupervised alone at home whilst they went out to buy drugs. The following is an example of this:

And scared because I left her in herself, even like during the day I would go away to score and I would think I would only be five minutes, know, and I probably wouldn't know this as well unless she [daughter] told me. One time my cousin came round to see me and she sat with the wean an hour and a half and that's how long I took but I didn't ever think I was that long, d'you know what I mean and she had to sit in for hours sometimes.

(Parent: Morgan)

This parent was not talking about a one-off situation. She was routinely leaving her child alone. When she worked in the town as a prostitute, she also left her in the house alone asleep. Even without adding in the drama of possible fires, or other dangers, one has only to imagine the terror of a young child waking up alone. There were also those parents who reported having left even younger children alone at home, locked in the house whilst they went to buy drugs. In the following case a social worker visited during the time the mother was out trying to buy drugs and had left her two-year-old son alone in the house:

> One morning I got up – Sam was sleeping right, and I was rattling. And I was like 'Oh no, I've got to wake him up and get through all this getting dressed carry on, get the clothes on and into the buggy and…'. So I was like that to myself 'If I went down and get a taxi and then straight back, he'd be sleeping.' So, I done that. He was sleeping by the time I got back and I was like 'that's alright then'. So the next morning, same thing happened. So I done it and the guy I went to never had any kit [heroin]. So I had to get a taxi five minutes down the road, but I was only away about 15 minutes maximum. I got to the door and the police were there, social workers and all that. I was like 'Oh my God.' They says the wean was at the door screaming and all that…

> (Parent: Mel)

This account was unusual in that a professional had discovered it. Most of the events the parents in the sample recounted had, in the main, gone either unreported or unnoticed, even when they were quite routine. At one level this is a failure of services to identify and monitor the situations of these families. Equally, however, one has to acknowledge the improbability that any service could be in a position to monitor this level of *potential* exposure to risk, particularly given that so many of these risky situations arose out of supervisory neglect. As Coohey (2003) has pointed out, supervisory neglect (as opposed for example to more concrete signs of neglect like, for example, a chronically dirty house) is one of the most difficult forms of neglect to monitor, because it requires someone to observe it precisely at the time that it is happening.

Having secured drugs, the moment of drug ingestion could also pose risks to children. Parents would exclude their children from bathrooms or kitchens whilst they administered their drugs, which might mean that children were left unsupervised for (often extended) periods of time. When parents are incapacitated by drugs they are unable to supervise children who can then be exposed to the many household hazards such as falling, being burnt or scalded, drinking dangerous substances:

> Well, I remember when Sam was a wee baby and I was holding him in my arms feeding him, I'd be gouching [fully under the drug effects] and the bottle would go up his nose or…I'd be just about to hit the floor with him…I think there was one time actually that I nearly dropped him.
>
> (Parent: Mel)

This parent and others, spoke of times when they had been 'gouching' or 'nodding' and had accidentally set quilts or blankets on fire with lit cigarettes. One mother, whose misuse of the sedative Temazepam had rendered her virtually unconscious, described a particularly frightening scenario involving her daughter:

> She would say 'watch Mum, you've got a fag' and stuff like that and maybe I'd be sitting too close to the fire, 'watch Mum' and like one time I went and fell asleep and I went and left a chip pan on and the place…the whole house full of smoke and the kitchen was on fire and she was the one that woke me up. …Know, the fire brigade and the ambulance and that said 'you were very lucky to get out of that' but she didn't move from the bed until she woke me up and I kept wakening up and going 'it's alright, just go back to sleep' and she was screaming the place down, but I got her out…
>
> (Parent: Morgan)

When one sets drug routines alongside childcare routines, it is difficult not to conclude that exposure to risk is an integral feature of these children's lives. Fundamental to this exposure to risk was the children's exposure to criminality; it is to this issue that attention now turns.

Children's exposure to criminality

The illegalities of heroin and other drug use entail close contact with an underworld of drug supply that operates at the margins of society. Drugs are expensive and most problem drug users find it difficult to meet the costs of an escalating habit through legitimate means. Shoplifting, prostitution and drug dealing were the most likely crimes to be reported in this study. Parents could not easily prevent exposing their children to the criminality associated with problem drug use, although some tried to prevent or limit the extent of this exposure. Again the success with which this could be achieved seemed to depend in large part on the part played by close relatives in shielding children from exposure. The following couple, for instance, described a hectic daily routine to fund their drug use that relied on the mothers' relatives to look after the baby:

> When he was a baby, aye, and we used to [go out shoplifting]…my younger sister, she used to watch him… Every day and we used to pay her…so it was only more or less in the morning we had him, know what I mean, 'til we were going out… Sometimes we weren't getting back 'til nine, ten o'clock at night, d'you know what I mean, so it was just more or less putting him to his bed and back up again…

(Parents: Hamish and Anna)

It was not always possible to leave children with relatives and indeed, there were those parents who acknowledged that taking a baby out in a pram provided good cover and a place to conceal stolen goods, older children were useful in this regard too:

> 'Cos I used to kind of a use her as well, so that I wouldn't get pulled by the police and things like that if I had her with me. But in saying that, I had been pulled a few times when she was with me, then Anita (her then seven or eight-year-old daughter)… she was like 'watch this mammy' and the police were going by and she started to wave and I went 'what are you doing?' She went 'they'll not think of anything if I'm waving to them' and I couldn't get over that…

(Parent: Faith)

Shoplifting was reported by virtually all parents in the sample at some point in their drug careers, as it provided a relatively painless means of securing income to pay for the drugs. Some parents reported becoming very proficient at it, however few had escaped being caught at least once. Where children were with parents this might entail them also being held in police custody with the parent until the child could be taken to the other partner or a relative. A more alarming scenario was reported where a father had been arrested for shoplifting and for fear of adding to the charges against him, had avoided reporting to police that he had left his two-year-old child alone at home.

Drug dealing too was common, often from the house, which meant that children could not easily escape exposure to drugs and other drug users. In these situations, children seem particularly vulnerable and it is probably no surprise that many of the children interviewed described being greatly disturbed by this flow of often strange and often rather frightening people, who, as one 11-year-old child described, were 'unsuitable people'.

I mean the two of us [parents] were doing the same, leaving the needles lying about and people were coming in and saying 'is it alright if I have a hit?' And 'aye, no bother, batter in, on you go' and that's just not right... Sometimes even the house would be full...I mean that's when you find out who your pals are, when you're selling drugs, everybody's all over you...

(Parent: Angela)

Drug dealing is obviously illegal and risks raids from police. Children were present when such drug raids took place and inevitably these caused alarm and distress. However these data suggest an altogether more frightening scenario where other drug users raided houses in which dealing was taking place. Using the threat of violence, sometimes through directly threatening violence to children, these predators would demand that money and drugs be handed over. Violence also broke out where money was owed to drug suppliers who came to collect payment by force if necessary. Children were often present at these events, which as described by their parents must have been deeply traumatic, particularly as in the following, not isolated, case where the child was used as a pawn:

Then, the house that I was staying in, the fella was selling heroin and we got robbed at knifepoint. Now the kids were there when this happened...the fellas that were robbing us, we knew them. This was 14 up [14th floor of a tower block] this happened, where we stayed, and they knew that there was heroin 18 up as well and they asked me to go up and chap [knock on] the door so the girl would open the door and I said 'no', so they grabbed my son Ethan with the knife and they got him to run up and chap the door but I ran with Ethan and I was saying you know 'get your hands off my baby' and all that and there was screaming going on and everything was going on and wee Ethan was screaming and I'm pulling Ethan and they were pulling Ethan and I'm saying 'get your hands off my son' and the wean chapped the door and I've grabbed him and ran right down the stairs with him.

(Parent: Nicky)

Without a doubt, the criminality associated with use of drugs such as heroin and cocaine, is an important aspect of these children's vulnerability since it exposes them to violence and to dangerous people. However it is not the whole of it. The heart of the problem for children is that they come second to their parents' relationship with drugs, and as a result they miss out on many of the most mundane, yet also the most valued, nurturing experiences. The next and final section comes full circle to the compulsivity at the heart of drug dependence, the resultant primary focus on drugs and what this meant in terms of the relationships parents felt able to have with them. 'Being there' was a term used and understood by parents and children to encompass a sense of a watchful, caring and providing presence and it was this that parental drug problems so eroded.

Not being there

> It's the needle. It's the habit. It's the whole making up of your hit and doing that, doing that thing: shutting the doors and sitting in front of the fire and all this… Then you feel, know how, you're injecting it in, you're injecting it into yourself and it's (sigh of relief) that kind of feeling… 'I'm alright now, everything's alright'.
>
> (Parent: Mel)

The absorbing attention to detail, the sense of delicious anticipation and focus, the promise of relief and comfort that this woman describes is riveting. This is a journey that is about her and the drug. It is like following a spotlight; everything outside of its sphere is in darkness. Outside of this focus, however, is Mel's son, who from birth until the age of two was with her through all her problem drug-using days. When these parents spoke of how drugs took 'everything away' from them they meant their capacity to feel, care and respond to their children or indeed anyone else:

> I didn't feel anything at the time because the drugs just, the drugs take all that away from you, you've no, you've no nothing, you've no feelings, no…you don't feel anything.
>
> (Parent: Faith)

Where do children fit in so arid a landscape? The emotional numbness that this parent describes has received relatively little attention and yet it is how this translates into an emotional unavailability that seems, by the accounts of parents and their children, to be most damaging. Drugs become so absorbing that they reduce parent–child relationships to being seen as burdensome obligations such that it is possible for a parent to say 'it's funny you don't really realize they're there…' (Ariana). Even those parents who considered that their drug problem was sufficiently under control not to compromise the safety of children had a sense of the emotional distance that drugs put between them.

I didn't sit and read to him at night. I didn't play with him with toys, I didn't colour in with him, I didn't do any of they kinda things. I didn't sit and talk to him. I didn't learn him how to talk.

(Parent: Ava)

A similar sense obtains from the following mother's description of how drugs got in the way of her relationship with her son:

'Cos if I'm lying on the couch strung out, I'll not want to do nothing with him and if I'm lying full of it, I'll lie and sleep so…I've not done much with him cause he's always wanting to do stuff, play games with you or something.

(Parent: Ashley)

It was the times when they were withdrawing from drugs that these parents reported being least able to attend to the needs of their children. These were times when tempers were most frayed and children were least tolerated.

As long as I had my drugs I was happy, so everything was all happy round about, that's the way I remember it but it probably wasn't. Probably chaotic for the wean, you know. I'm thinking like 'och I'm fine' you know what I mean, once I was full of it, brand new and all that, but the wean must've known like the mood swings were going up and down, one minute Mammy's wanting to play with you all happy and the next minute she's 'GRRR', screaming at you, running you up the hall and throwing you in your room, know what I mean, and shut the door, 'STAY THERE, 'til I get something', know what I mean and then once you got it you were like that [calm] and the wean must've been 'how is she alright now? About an hour ago she was wanting to kill me.'

(Parent: Julia)

Such dramatic oscillations between mood states, because unpredictable, must been alarming, confusing and a source of anxiety, particularly for younger children who could not 'read' their parents with any certainty and were never sure when and what would next trigger anger and conflict in the house. One effect on children would be to keep out of the way of parents, to keep quiet and do what they were told. This mother now recovering from her drug problem recalled how she stressed to her daughter the importance of her not impinging upon her:

R: I was quite controlling as well.

I: In what sense?

R: Well I think I sort of always stressed to her not to annoy me, not to cry. Not to demand from me, to be good and try and say as little as possible and do what she was told. And if she done that everything would be fine 'cos I can't cope with anything other than that so I was very controlling.

(Parent: Hilary)

The overriding sense one gets from these descriptions is of children who are sidelined by their parents' relationship with drugs. The best they seemed to be able to hope for was the small window of time when their parents' drug intake had reached a plateau allowing them to operate on a relatively even keel. It was at these times that parents were most likely to attend to their children:

But that part inside me also knew that this is wrong…it was just a feeling that 'there is good in you Gill' but I don't know how to show it and I think that was the part of me that parented Layla at times, that says 'this is what you should be doing, you should be giving your wee baby cuddles, you should be sitting playing a wee game with your baby, you should be doing these things' and it was only when I was full of it that I could try, know, to perform these things but it would all go away because drugs was always there.

(Parent: Gill)

Drugs so fettered her relationship with her daughter that it was the exception not the norm to hold and play with her or to take much pleasure in the process. This sense of emotional disconnectedness was characterized similarly by many other parents and was part and parcel of the overwhelming experience of parenting whilst also in the midst of a drug dependency problem.

Conclusion

The argument that need and risk are intrinsic potentials where a parent with a drug problem has responsibility for children is a strong one. The prevalent operational presumption of the recent past *not* to anticipate problems with childrearing just because that parent has a drug problem runs counter to the conclusions reached by this research.

We do not help parents, or indeed their children, if we fail fully to recognize, and address the potential for drug problems to compromise parental capacity. This is not an issue confined to agencies charged with social welfare for children and families, but for any agency dealing with problem drug users. Where someone has a drug problem and is a parent, their children have to be taken into consideration. Never far away is the fear for parents that children will be taken away from their care. For some professionals that fear has been enough to prevent discussion of their clients' children so as not to compromise the therapeutic relationship with the adult. The stark truth of course is that child protection is a part of the equation whether or not the issue is skirted because uncomfortable or threatening.

In these interviews it was the parents whose drug problems were in the past, or currently more under control, who were best able to consider the negative impact of their lifestyle on their children. If part of the problem for parents in the midst of their dependency problems is that their narrow focus on drugs has prevented them from seeing the effects of their drug use on their children, it must surely be part of the responsibility of agencies in engaging with their clients to help them see and do something about it. This does not have to be a punitive undertaking; most parents want the best for their children but this can get lost where drugs have become so preoccupying. Encouraging a wider focus can be part of the process of recovery because it disturbs the primacy of the relationship with drugs. Both in this and other research (McIntosh and McKeganey 2001) there were parents whose children became the prime motivation for stabilizing or getting off drugs. The positive part that a child might play in a parent's recovery from drugs is, however, secondary to the point that, whilst parents continue to use drugs problematically, their children are at elevated risk of harm. Preventing that harm must start with recognition that it is embedded within the illegalities and compulsiveness of a drug problem. The policy and practice implications of so emphatic an argument are discussed in Chapter 10, which deals with the adequacy of current policy and service responses to drugs in the family as a whole.

Chapter 6

Children Growing Up with Parents who have Drug Problems

For all that they did to us 'cos of the drugs, they were our mum and dad and we knew that they loved us and we were scared of being separated from them and going into foster care.

(Rachel)

Introduction

When we are children, our parents, whoever they are and whatever they do, are at the centre of our world. Through our primary caregivers we learn to understand and make sense of the world. We look to them for security, reassurance and certainty and when we get it, we develop a sense of our own importance, a sense of the value of others and a deep seated confidence that the world is a safe, reliable and caring place, where we feel loved and liked and, in return, trust enough to love and like others (Howe 2005). What does the world look like to the child whose parents are unable to provide consistent care, security and reassurance and whose responsiveness is greatly impeded by a preoccupation with problem drug use? Importantly too, what does that lack mean for the development of the child? This chapter looks at what children and young people had to say about their parents and their use of drugs and how they affected their lives.

One might have thought that the children and young people who were interviewed for this study would have talked at length, and in the most graphic terms, of the impact their parents' drug use had on their lives: in fact, it was often difficult for them to put into words their experiences. When one considers the enormity of what was being asked of them, this is perhaps less surprising than it might look at first sight. The parents of these children, whatever their failings, were the bedrock of their children's lives. They were quite literally the people upon whom these children depended, even in the face of the neglect they often experienced, and it is for this reason that the children and young people did not always find it easy to talk about their family lives to an outsider, even where their own parents had encouraged them to do so. Often the greatest concern was for the child who said the least.

Through the silences and elisions of some, the fractured hesitancy and the flow and eloquence of others, this chapter offers an imperfect glimpse of childhoods lived in the shadow of drugs. The first section of this chapter describes the 36 children and young people who participated in the 'Growing up in drug dependent households' study (Barnard *et al.* 2000). Carrying out these interviews was a great challenge; children and young people living in such households are busy keeping the family secret because their parent's drug problem is shaming and they are afraid of being removed from parental care. Parents too can be afraid; they are fearful of losing their children and feel unease over what children know and what they might say. The impulse to keep the family situation hidden from view means that such children are difficult to contact and find it difficult to openly acknowledge their experience of growing up in their families.

The 36 young people and children

As far as possible, the aim was to contact children and young people, aged eight and over, who lived with one or both of their parents. This accounted for 27/36 children interviewed. The remaining nine young people interviewed (aged 15–17) no longer lived with their parents. Most of these nine young people had quite pronounced social and emotional difficulties of their own. Four were in a secure unit for young people on account either of their involvement in criminality or under 'place of safety' orders (Children Act [Scotland] 1995) because of their drug use and involvement in prostitution. A further four were resident in a drug rehabilitation unit for adolescents. These young people manifested troubled behaviours. However, the family backgrounds they described were not very different to those of some of the other children and young people interviewed who were still living with their parents.

In the face of the difficulties in finding children and young people who would talk about these aspects of their lives, the research strategy to sample purposively, across the birth order and equally between genders etc., had to adapt to the reality that the sample would be opportunistic. In the event, the most likely child to be interviewed was the eldest, and more females than males agreed to be interviewed (20:16). It was most likely that they would be older in years too. Partly this was because younger children (8–10 years) were the least likely to agree to be interviewed and were least likely, or able, to speak about parental drug use; indeed they may not have reached this understanding at this age. Where drug use was not mentioned of the child's own accord, the researchers did not mention it either. There were four young boys (8–9 years) who did not make any mention of parental drug use. In the case of two, this might have been because they did not know; the remaining two boys did know, according to their parents, because of the specificity of their exposure to their drug problems.

The average age of the young people interviewed was 14.8 years and ranged from 8 to 22 years (12 children were aged 12 and under; 19 were aged 13–17 years and 5 were aged 19–22). These latter were obviously young adults and for ease of reference are incorporated in the generic term 'children and young people', throughout, although the age of each respondent will be indicated.

From here on the chapter focuses on describing, firstly, the children and young people's understanding of their parents drug problem and its effect on their home lives and, secondly, the ways in which they felt it had affected them and their view of the world.

Discovering parental drug use

It is impossible to be categorical about the age at which parental drug use became 'known' about by children and young people. Some reported having known about drugs from a very early age (the earliest was at about four years). However, the interviews suggest that most pieced together an awareness that illegal drugs were part of the family dynamic between 10 and 12 years of age. This was usually preceded by the strong sense that something was 'going on' in the household, even whilst not necessarily being able to name it. A good example of this can be heard in the following interview extract from an 11-year-old girl, whose mother had recently told her about her father's drug problem, which finally explained her father's strange behaviour:

> He always told me to keep out of the living room. That made me...angry that he didn't want me being with him...I kept asking my mum questions...'How come my dad doesn't let me in the living room?' Or, if he did like me or not? And my dad came in and my dad and my mum says that he took drugs... I just went into my bedroom and started crying.
>
> (Child of problem drug-using father: Simone, 11 years)

Her puzzlement, and her anger over being excluded from his company, led to her mother taking the decision to tell her. Most of the other children and young people interviewed made the connection by themselves, as no one explained. Among the parents interviewed, for example, only two said that they had directly told their children about their drug use. For the most part, parents acknowledged great ambivalence as to the merits of broaching the subject, partly to protect them and partly because there was no easy way to frame it. Where drug use was referred to at all it would mostly be couched in medical terms, although this explanation would not necessarily be accepted. The cues for most children seemed to be their parents' behaviours, which would alter dramatically between being 'moanie' and bad-tempered to being quiet, even-tempered and drowsy, usually after a private, and often long, visit to the kitchen or bathroom. Tin foil; blackened spoons; the smell of citric acid were also associated with this transformation.

> I could tell, like it was just the way she gouched, she was sitting on the couch and she would gouch and she wouldn't wake up, oh, the way her eyes were, and the way she talked. The tone and all that. And just the way she went. She started going funny, she didn't go, she wasn't the way she used to be. She was different...
>
> (Child of drug-using parent: Jenny, 15 years)

About half of young people and children reported that they had walked in on one, or both, of their parents when they were in the process of using drugs:

> I walked in on them once when I was a wee boy and I saw them [my mum, aunt and uncle] taking stuff... Aye, and other people that were in the house taking it...taking drugs...like on tinfoil...tooting... That's the first time I caught them and they just...they started doing it in front of me, didn't hide it then... I could just tell it was drugs 'cos I could hear people talking about it and that.
>
> (Child of problem drug-using parent: Dan, 15 years)

Even having witnessed the event, it could still be difficult knowledge to fully grasp as is apparent from the following account where Susan described having shied away from 'knowing' what she had seen:

> When my Mum started to sell like our Christmas stuff that we had got, like my CD player, my wee brother's Playstation... Stuff like that...I saw them taking it [drugs]... Both of them...I didn't know what it was but I knew in a way 'cause they used to tell me it was 'Askits' but I knew, like, deep inside. I was thinking, on top of me, 'aye it is' but if they were

taking it nearly all the time, I knew it wasn't. There was a lot of people coming in saying 'do you want...', know how there's different names for it? And they were saying 'do you want this' and things like that... I just clicked, aye...I mean I must've been about...about, phew, I'm 14 the now...I was about ten.

(Child of problem drug-using parents: Susan, 14 years)

These lucid accounts of discovering, or understanding, that drugs were a part of the family circumstance are counterbalanced by the difficulties some had in talking at all about their parent's drug use. Looking for example at the following account provided by a socially withdrawn teenage boy who had suffered many long spells of separation from his mother, affirms the burden of knowing, and of sharing that knowledge. In spite of his mother's full encouragement to open up, he simply could not articulate his experience, to the researchers or indeed anyone else, although he acknowledged in the briefest of terms that her drug problem made him angry and left him feeling helpless. In the following account he denies any direct knowledge of his mother's drug use:

I: Right, okay. Do you know what kind of drugs your mum uses? Can you tell me what they are?

R: Aye, heroin.

I: Right. How do you know that?

R: 'Cause I know what it looks like, I've seen it on the telly.

I: Right, right. Have you ever seen her using it?

R: No.

(Child of drug-using parent: Niall, 15 years)

Contrast this then with his mother's account of the strong upset he displayed when she felt compelled to inject in front of him:

Justine said that Niall had actively witnessed her drug use and she described having injected in front of him twice. 'He wouldn't leave the room, just stayed sitting and so in the end I did it in front of him whilst he just sat there, the tears rolling down his face. I just said "I'm sorry son, you know mammy's sick, you should have gone out of the room, I had to do it."'

(Justine, Niall's mother)

This young man's resistance is as telling as the eloquence of others. It underscores the significance of their parents in their lives and draws attention to their deep-seated anxieties over their parents' drug problems and its profound impact on them and their home environment. It is to these that attention next turns.

Living with the elephant in the room

Whilst not necessarily understanding much about drugs, younger children were nonetheless caught in their gravitational pull, and had to make sense of their own place in homes dominated by something that might only be imperfectly grasped. Those children who had come to understand that drugs were the problem were at least clear on that. Of course this knowledge would not make their households any more predictable or less confusing:

> I think it was about 10 or 11…when I realized that my Mum was different from others… She was just always dead moody, she was always in her bed all the time and, like, she would never go out and buy food and she would never have money to go out and buy it. 'Em, like she was living with her ex-partner at the time and she was always arguing with him about not having any money and, about, like, not having any food and not tidying up and things like that. There would be big massive fights about it…it got to be violent.
>
> (Child of problem drug-using parent: Katy, 20 years)

These children and young people's accounts depicted households that were in a constant state of flux, largely due to a high degree of parental responsivity to their own drug-related needs. Children perceived that drugs meant that their parents were very busy and preoccupied, which made it hard for them to attract their attention:

> She would always be doing something…she'd be like, 'Oh I can't talk to you the now, I've got to do this and I've got to do that kind of thing…
>
> (Child of problem drug-using parent: Susan, 14 years)

The likelihood that drug routines would prevail over childcare routines was apt to result in unpredictable mealtimes, bedtimes, erratic school attendance and a general lack of supervision and parental care:

> I just looked after myself… I just went out every morning, just went through and got money off my ma every morning, she used to give us money all the time and I'd just go out with my pals and that, I'd just do

what I wanted, go in for my dinner or just go in and get money and go out for my dinner…I just went out all the time.

(Child of problem drug-using parent: Nigel, 16 years)

The absorption of household monies into paying for drugs could, and often did, result in little money being available for food, heating and clothing.

There were a few times we didn't have electricity and our door was boarded up and it was just pulled off the sides and you just had to go in and sit with candles… We didn't really have much at all, there was a few times there wasn't any food at all but I think I lived on pieces [sandwiches] and chocolate spread for ages.

(Child of problem drug-using parent: Orla, 19 years)

Another outcome would be unpaid mounting debt that further underscored the instability of these children's living circumstances. Unpaid rent could mean eviction and moving house, as might unpaid debts for drug bills. These children reported a good deal of transience not just to different parts of their hometown but all over the country. Some children were unable to list all the primary schools they had attended; some had big gaps where they did not go to school at all. The effect on those children and young people who had experienced this amount of disturbance was often anxiety:

[I've moved] about eight times…went to eight different schools. Whenever I went into a school, they'd either be like behind me or ahead of me, so I'd either have to wait for them or catch up or stuff like that, 'em, with my work but I found it hard having to make new pals all the time, really, I couldn't handle that, it was just pure nerve-wracking every time I went to a new school.

(Child of problem drug-using parent: Beth, 19 years)

The following boy greatly resented the life he had lived as a result of his mother's drug problem, particularly the constant moving he had endured and the lack of schooling which had resulted in him missing three years of school and meant that he now had to attend a special school:

I think that's what made me have a bad temper… My mum, 'cos of going through all of that and things… All the moving about and things like that… And not going to school.

(Child of problem drug-using parent: Dan, 15 years)

He, like others, had also been exposed to traumatic events, often in the shape of drug-related violence involving other predatory drug users, as well as police drug raids. These could be terrifying, as in his following dramatic account:

> These guys who used to buy stuff off my uncle, they all burst in and were holding knives up to our throats and that, asking for the drugs and the money and they were saying that they'd slit our throats if they didn't give them it.
>
> (Child of problem drug-using parent: Dan, 15 years)

It was also clear that the houses these children and young people lived in often hosted some frightening people, exacerbated by the children witnessing the alarming drug induced states some got into at their homes.

Separation from parents

Separation from parents was commonly experienced (Kolar *et al.* 1994). Frequent, sudden, often unexplained and prolonged absences by parents who went in search of drugs or money were a source of great distress for children and young people. These disappearances for unspecified periods of time were puzzling and anxiety-provoking, even when they were left with relatives or friends:

> I didn't see her as much and like she didn't always have a lot of money and she was always like rushing about and tired and stuff. My brothers they didn't see her as much either, they were always with my auntie… And they used to always wonder where she was…
>
> (Child of drug-using parent: Sarah, 14 years)

In the above family, the children were not usually unattended but left with either their aunt or granny, although sometimes they were left with people they did not know. These disappearances were experienced as deeply unsettling. They could not rely on their mother to be around, they did not know where she was going, or for how long and they worried what would happen to her. As the following young woman described these disappearances could last for days:

> I was always like the grown up when I was small, like the mother, I would cook for my brother, I would clean the house, and, like, my mum would be out burgling and she'd lose track of time, she'd come back and she'd say…I'd say, 'Oh you said you were only going to be a couple of hours and you've been three days', and she be like, 'What are you on about, I've only been a couple of hours' and you know, no track of time

whatsoever and I couldn't understand that but now, with using myself, I can understand exactly... The longest stretch on my own was a week.

(Child of drug-using parent: Ruth, 17 years)

Unsurprisingly, children and young people experienced being left alone at home as disturbing and frightening:

I wouldn't have minded if I was with her all the time, but she used to leave me in the house and all that myself for hours and hours and I just used to greet [cry] and that's when I felt scared in case anything, anybody came up to the door or anything like that but...I'd just watch the telly... I must have been about nine.

(Child of drug-using parent: Orla, 19 years)

Had they been known about, both instances illustrated above would have been significant child protection concerns. The emotional vulnerability engendered as a result of such unstable patterns of parental contact is just as significant. The following child's description of his disappointment that neither parent consistently comes to see him in foster care is a depressingly flat statement of his low expectations that they will turn up, or even really understand the importance of the visit to him:

At the moment I see my mum every week but sometimes my mum doesn't turn up... And the same goes for my dad... I meet them in the social work office... She just says she forgot, or, she had to see somebody. I tell her that it makes me feel sad. She says, 'Sorry, son'... That's it.

(Child of drug-using parent: Richard, 10 years)

'Hundreds of hurt'

When my mum is using drugs it just makes me feel as if I am here myself – not got anyone else here.

(Child of drug-using parents: Jenny, 15 years)

Living in homes where nothing was very certain was a key feature of all the descriptions provided by those children and young people who named parental drug problems as an issue. These accounts whilst replete with disruption, separation and uncertainty, were centred on their core feeling that their parents' relationship with drugs excluded them from their rightful place at the heart of their parent's lives. The one exception to this was a 15-year-old girl whose mother had not developed a drug problem until she was ten years old. The mother had run an initially highly successful drug dealing business that had shielded her children from being involved in having to find and fund drugs:

> My Mum, she cooked a meal everyday, she had our school uniforms ready, she had our breakfast ready for when we got up, she was always there for birthdays, Christmas, pick us up from school and... She was just like a normal mum to me...she was never really off her face to me...I think there's been about three times I've seen her like that.
>
> (Child of problem drug-using parent: Karen, 14 years)

Karen considered that her mother's drug problem had never resulted in her being sidelined. However, Karen's reported initiation into heroin injecting at the age of 11 indicates the presence of serious problems. For the rest of the children and young people, it was this feeling of not coming first that was most damaging. They could not rely on their parents to provide them with what they needed, when they needed it. This was an issue for children and young people, and was closely tied to their sense of what it meant to be properly cared for. Indeed one 16-year-old boy described periods where his mother had a lot of money through drug dealing but he did not value it because the material wealth was an offshoot of having a mother on drugs:

> She got us everything, I had about seven computers, man, I had everything but it was nothing really, I just didn't want it, I just wanted a better life for her...
>
> (Child of problem drug-using parent: Nigel, 15 years)

Similarly, Jane considered that her mother's drug problem did not deprive her of anything material, or, left her vulnerable to harm. Her expressed problem with her mother was perhaps diffuse, but deeply felt:

> It annoys me and it makes me feel dead hurt, I feel as if I just want to batter her... The way she just sits about and all that, when she's full of it and she just annoys me and she...like a pure idiot man...I pure hate it when she does it and then she tried to deny it and that's one of the worst things I hate about her...
>
> (Child of problem drug-using parent: Jane, 14 years)

Food and clean clothing were important, but less so than someone who was interested, who would talk to them, take notice of them, ask about school, come to see them in the school play; those smaller yet significant markers of responsiveness and care:

> There was once at my Christmas play, oh it was ages ago and my auntie had came 'cos like my mum and dad never, and I was looking all about for them 'cos they said they would come and they never… I thought they must not care about me then…things like racing, like your school sports, and they said they would come to that but they never…it was just, when I think about it now, it was like heartbreaking.

> (Child of problem drug-using parent: Susan, 14 years)

That drugs so got in the way of their parents' ability to care for them seemed the hardest thing to live with, and its legacy of disappointment, sadness and anger was deep-rooted and long lasting. Even in those few families where the parent's drug problem was kept in reasonable check, in this case apparently because of the control exerted by the father who did not have a drug problem, children reported their absolute aversion to the use of drugs by one or both of their parents:

> I want her to do it, stop using drugs…well how much can I say? I can't say how much 'cos it's the most in the whole world. You can't really say a number can you?

> (Child of problem drug-using parent: Jane, 14 years)

Time and time again, these children and young people referred to their expectations of parental relationships of care and protection, and how significant the lack of it was to them. For example, this 13-year-old girl describes her understanding of what parental boundaries signal in terms of feeling cared for:

> What I hate most is she'll not be like a normal ma and she'll not be, like, alert and all that to watch after you 'cos you want a ma that'll just give you rules and all that, it's not something all the weans want… But it's annoying sometimes, just being able to do what you want because people say to you 'your ma doesn't care about you, she lets you go out to whatever time you want'… I want her to be… Just be like a normal ma, if you do something wrong, you'll get shouted at or grounded or something.

> (Child of drug-using parent: Leonie, 13 years)

Children did not accept their circumstances willingly and would express it through argument as in the following description:

> I used to feel angry like when my mum was on drugs 'cos I used to think how could this have happened to me, it was just sad all the time and then I would get angry...and we would have arguments all the time...
>
> (Child of drug-using parent: Anita, 11 years)

This anger might be expressed through breaking things, as the following young boy described:

> I just used to get angry, just sit in my room. I had all these toys and I just used to just hit them down...and my mum had just fixed them and she used to come in and fix them again. And I used to knock them down again.
>
> (Child of drug-using parent: Andy, 12 years)

His rage, as he described it, was confined to smashing his own toys, which in a sense underlines the relative powerlessness to change things that he and many of the other young people attested to:

> You can't do nothing about it, you can't go...leave home or nothing, you just can't say that's not right, you can't be doing that, 'I'm not for any of that', you can't say that... 'Cos like a ten-year-old saying that, you wouldn't say that...
>
> (Child of drug-using parent: Susan, 14 years)

After all, as children, what options were really open to them? Telling someone could lead to being taken away from parents which could seem an unimaginably daunting prospect. It was a fear that some parents apparently played on, and which had the effect of locking them further into silence:

> But like if you go like that 'I don't want to stay here' and all that – but you do want to stay with her, you just don't want to stay with her the way she is, you want her to get better and all that – and then she does that 'Aye well you know what to do' and all that, meaning go up to the social work and put yourself in care and all that... You do want to stay with her when you say that, it's just you don't want to stay with her like that, you want her to be a 'normal' ma... The longest she's been like that is about a month.
>
> (Child of drug-using parent: Leonie, 13 years)

As Leonie makes clear, going into care was not the outcome that she (or other of these children and young people) wanted, although in two cases when it did occur, it was described as being a relief to be out of the immediate situation. However simplistic the notion they wanted to have their parent; the person that they felt existed outside of drugs. They held onto this sense of their parent, but were wounded by the distance between this and the lives they and their parents lived because of drugs:

> I mean I always felt dead close to her, I felt as if I was pure hurting inside because I didn't want to see her like that all the time, and falling asleep and everybody thinking the worst of her and all that...when I done things in school, it used to be, phew, well, nobody cares, my ma doesn't care, so...
>
> (Child of drug-using parent: Orla, 19 years)

They forgave them their problems, and although often disappointed in their expectations, they worked hard to try to understand how drugs affected their behaviour. The following young woman had lived in foster and residential care since the age of five. Through all of this time she held on to her hope of being reconciled with her mother, her loyalty was steadfast even as she recounted her mother's affirmation that she worked as a prostitute:

> I says, 'you're my ma at the end of the day and I still love you, no matter what you do. If that's what you want to do, phew, it's not up to me'.
>
> (Child of drug-using parent: Elise, 14 years)

Yet, at the same time, she acknowledged the toll her mother's drug problem had exacted, she felt unwanted and this greatly affected her sense of her own worth:

> I don't know, why I started heroin... It was just...me thinking nobody cares about me, I'm in fucking care, no family to go to, to stay with, I've not even got a fucking normal life.
>
> (Child of problem drug-using parent: Elise, 14 years)

These interviews oscillated notably between awareness of their own losses and the mix of anger, sadness and hopelessness this engendered, to a prevailing, sometimes overwhelming, sense of worry and anxiety as to the welfare of the mother. The following young woman perfectly illustrates this in describing her younger brother's behaviour:

> I mean she never ever gave them a decent life, and I mean Jim, he is 16 now. His childhood nearly over and nothing to show for it... It's not as if he's had a normal upbringing. I feel as if he's always been worried about my mum – he's got a lot of anger in him because of it. He's always

just been dead angry... Every time she went to the toilet Jim used to stand outside the toilet door...to see what she was doing.

(Child of problem drug-using parent: Katy, 20 years)

This worry resulted in hypervigilance around the house to try to stop the mother using drugs, or to watch for signs of overdose. This tendency for children to become overly responsible, not just for the parents welfare, but also in taking on parental roles with other children, was very commonly described in these accounts.

Taking charge of the household

The worst thing about my childhood? I think the fact it was as if she was the child and I was the mum, it was the way it was kind of reversed.

(Child of drug-using parent: Beth, 19 years)

A consequence of having parents whose drug problems were overriding was that children had to fend for themselves. Of course, where young children were concerned the lack of parental oversight could leave them highly vulnerable, as in the description provided by the following child who at the age of eight had roamed wild with his younger brother:

I went to live with my foster-carer because my mum didn't look after us properly and she didn't have a house and she didn't know what we were doing at night and things...me and my young brother we were stealing out the Asda, 'em, smashing windows and not listening to what my mum was saying... She was all different places, my gran's, she would go out places, to friends... When I was living with my mum I was just running about...

(Child of problem drug-using parent: Richard, 10 years)

Elder siblings were most likely to have to take on responsibility for many aspects of care for their younger brothers and sisters:

I was looking after my wee brothers as well, quite a lot...just when Simon was a toddler, just feeding him or changing him and every time I went out...I had to take him as well so...I minded it... Sometimes...I must have been about ten. I would say the majority of the time I was looking after my brothers...

(Child of problem drug-using parent: Beth, 19 years)

Like many young carers generally, this was a role they came to occupy not out of choice but because there was, to their minds, no other option. This felt obligation to care could arise out of concern for the wellbeing of the younger sibling, as in the following case:

> Know how, like my ma was taking stuff and all that and the social work didn't really know and I'd be left with Will [her 3-year-old brother] and all that and I had to like take care of him and all that... And like my pals, they'd come up for me and I just wouldn't go out to play 'cos I was scared for my wee brother and that, what would happen like if she dropped her fag or something because she's nearly set the house alight with her fag I don't know how many times...
>
> (Child of problem drug-using parent: Leonie, 13 years)

It was however a source of resentment for some, often they felt ill equipped to meet the demands placed on them:

> I felt angry about having to look after him. It was just that, you've not got a wean or nothing like that and it's only your brother and you're left to watch him...we just ate cereal...
>
> (Child of problem drug-using parent: Lara, 15 years)

Taking on the caring role and therefore being responsible curtailed their ability to play, which again could lead to argument:

> Like there was bigger arguments about her always going out... If I wanted to go to my pals and she said I'd have to watch [my brothers] then I'd start arguing with her about that...I'd say I'm not watching them and she'd say stuff and make you feel pure guilty and then she would just go out.
>
> (Child of problem drug-using parent: Sarah, 15 years)

The burden of caring was not limited to their siblings, however. Their sense of responsibility extended to the parent with the drug problem. They understood that drugs made their parents vulnerable and made many efforts to counter this.

Caring for the parent

Looking out for, and looking after, the parent was universal in these data. Fear was at the heart of their concerns. They were afraid that their parents would be harmed by the drugs and afraid of the associated harms like setting fires when incapacitated, of drug related violence, of the consequences of criminality. Inevitably these fears were closely tied to their own anxieties as to the consequences for them if harm were to come to parents who might then no longer be able to look after them. They were therefore very apt to become their parent's protectors.

Drug misuse can be very frightening for children to witness. Children and young people reported being alarmed at seeing how drug withdrawal affected their parents:

> Sometimes I'd see her and she'd be pure white, know, just like a pure ghost, it was frightening...I'd go like that 'Mum what's wrong with you?' and she'd say 'nothing, just leave me alone the now' and she'd go out. And then she'd come back and she'd go like that, 'I'm sorry hen' and she'd be all nicey nice, know, that must've been after she had her hit or whatever.
>
> (Child of drug-using parent: Angela, 19 years)

To protect them from the pain of withdrawals, there were children who would offer to go in search of money or drugs for parents to make them better. Their great fear was that parents would overdose. Such anxiety was well founded given that research has consistently indicated its high prevalence among problem drug users (Neale 1999). The fear of harm created a pervasive anxiety that followed them through their day. Many of these children and young people had witnessed the occurrence of overdose in relatives, including their own parents. One can only imagine the trauma of the very young child attempting to respond to a mother's overdose, as in the following case, which occurred whilst resident in a homeless hostel:

> My ma kind of took a drug overdose but I didn't know, I just thought she was sleeping 'cos I was only six or something, five or six, didn't know any better and my wee sister was screaming and when I was younger I was like the ma of the family, I was always taking care of everybody. So I was trying to keep my wee sister quiet and trying to waken my ma up and I couldn't help her so I phoned down to the office and they got social workers up and they took me to respite carers to start with and they were horrible...
>
> (Child of problem drug-using parents: Elise, 14 years)

Some had also seen its fatal consequences. Take for example Kylie, who by the time she was 14 years old had lost three of her uncles through fatal overdose, one of whom she herself had discovered dead:

> It was Christmas morning and I was getting up to go to the toilet and I couldn't get in the door because he [uncle] was against the door and from then I realized something had happened to him...and I ran down the stair and I got my big brother and the two of us went up and we

eventually got the door opened and he was lying, his face pure chalk white, his lips were pure…he was yellow and his lips were bluish with blood and sick round his nose and his needle lying beside him, he'd just been out the jail a week…

(Child of drug-using parent: Kylie, 14 years)

In an effort to prevent risk of overdose, children reported that they would often stay by their parents until they came to, as with this young boy who described trying to waken his mother, as much as anything to protect her from being found in that state by her violent husband:

It was when we stayed in Blackhill, she was always dead sleepy… I can remember one time she was falling asleep and I tried to wake her up but she wouldn't wake up so I went in and I got my Walkman and I put it in her ears and I put it up full blast then she jumped up…

(Child of problem drug-using parent: Andy, 12 years)

The sense of watchfulness engendered in these children and young people was acute, and is not really surprising when one considers that their fates were so inextricably bound to those of their parents. Picture the following, for example, as this young woman listens outside the kitchen door for the signs that her mother has not overdosed from drugs:

I just used to have this fear that she was going to die, there would be a rocking chair at the kitchen and I remember times when I could hear the rocking chair rocking and that's when she'd be sat down injecting and she'd sit on the rocking chair.

(Child of problem drug-using parent: Ruth, 17 years)

In order to protect parents, there were children who reported staying off school, to watch out for them and sometimes with the specific aim of stopping them from taking drugs:

And just I used to stay off to make sure my ma didn't get drugs and all that… 'Cos I hate it…I used to follow her and not let her do it…I mean, like, I would make sure she stayed in the house with me… She wanted me to stay off and all but…so I could like…so I didn't let her take them.

(Child of problem drug user: Jane, 15 years)

In parenting her mother, Jane, like other of these young people, may have derived some pleasure from being in a relationship of care. However this has to be counterbalanced by their ambivalence over such an inversion of care based on the meeting of their parent's needs at the cost of suppressing their own. It is not surprising, therefore, that those such children should also express anger and anxiety in becoming overly responsible in the face of their parent's abdication of that role (Howe 2005).

Where a parent's drug problem came into calmer waters it was of course more possible for them to resume, or assume, some of these responsibilities and it is to this subject that the next section is addressed.

Relapse and rehabilitation

The dearest wish of these children and young people was that their mothers and/or fathers would become drug free, or at least stable on methadone. This was strongly allied to their wish for their parents to be 'normal' and therefore able to take on their care. They squarely placed the blame for their lives on drugs and, with the exception of a couple of young people, who, at least at that time, had lost faith, retained a vision of what their parents could be without drugs and a hope that they would achieve it. For some of the children, this hope had become a reality and one can plainly see in their contrasting accounts how greatly they appreciated the difference:

> 'Cos she's changed... She's doing stuff now, she's like getting things sorted, getting a house and, 'em, all kinds of stuff, just lots of things... She's like totally different, she's always, like, asking me where I'm going and when I'll be back and caring for me better than when she stayed in Drumchapel...I like that better...caring for me, like by not doing drugs anymore, she's caring about me that way, if you know what I mean.
>
> (Child of problem drug-using parent: Andy, 11 years)

This young boy had never doubted his mother's love for him but he understood how, in her preoccupation with drugs, there had been little interest in the everyday currency of his care. For Orla, the end of her mother's drug problem signalled the beginning of her taking the reins to care for them both:

> I just seen a big change in her when she stopped using, like she started going out and buying messages [shopping] and all that kind of thing... And being more responsible... Aye, she started, aye, even though I still cleaned and cooked and that kind of thing but it was a lot better... I was 12 then.
>
> (Child of problem drug-using parent: Orla, 19 years)

For Sarah, it was only once her mother became drug free and had fully assumed parental responsibility that her world began to seem more a reliable and less fraught place, leaving her the space 'to get on with other things' that were probably more age appropriate:

> It's better because my ma's alright and she's well and all that... So I can get on with other things... I know what's she's like... She's very honest, like she can tell me stuff... Things that she couldn't tell me before... Like, when she was taking drugs she would never tell me where she was going but now she always tells me everywhere she's going, when she'll be back, how long she's going for... See I never knew what was going to happen to her but I was too scared to talk to anybody.
>
> (Child of problem drug-using parent: Sarah, 14 years)

Children considered that their homes became happier places once drugs were out of the equation, importantly, too, there was less to frighten them in the shape of strange people, illegal activity and incipient violence:

> Now...well, I think it's happier because everybody's not shouting and they're not all angry and my mum's always happy rather than a sad and angry face on her all the time and it's always reasonable people that come in here, it's never people that I don't like.
>
> (Child of problem drug-using parent: Anita, 11 years)

One has to keep in mind that, for most, the journey to a drug-free life or stability is a rocky one with many hitches and slips along the way. These lapses were difficult for children and each one potentially eroded their confidence that this time their parent would manage to become free of the hold that illegal drugs had over them:

> I think he will stop using, and, I think he won't...because he says he will stop it then he starts again so I kind of believe him that he'll stop it, and I know that he will go back to it... I watch him to see... If he'll keep his promise, if he'll stop it...I feel sad...when he goes back to it...confused... That he says he gets off it and he goes back and he keeps his promises and then he says he doesn't... And it just annoys me... Like I just keep away from him sometimes, I really don't want to be around him with my mum.
>
> (Child of problem drug-using parent: Simone, 11 years)

In the face of many disappointments it was inevitably difficult for some children to trust that this time it really would be different and in this context one can see that children needed to defend themselves against the pain of having their hopes dashed again when their parents relapsed into drug use.

For many parents, the struggle to become drug free was rooted in their sense of wanting to do it for their children's sake, because they recognized the harm it was causing them. For the children, the articulation of such motivation could be read as a powerful indication of their parents' love:

> I'll be there for my mum all the way... She's coming off drugs to get me back... That makes me feel good 'cos I know that my mum's going to go through a really, really hard time just to get me back.
>
> (Child of problem drug-using parent: Shelley, 12 years)

Yet this could lead to greater disappointment where a parent relapsed. Dan, unlike his younger sister Shelley, would no longer tie his fortunes to the hope that, this time, their mother would become drug free. He had opted to stay with his grandma whatever the outcome, because there he felt safe and was sure that things would remain the same:

> I prefer it here 'cos when I go to my mum I don't like the people she hangs about with and things like that...and my gran doesn't hang about with anybody here, I just go out and play here...
>
> (Child of problem drug-using parent: Dan, 15 years)

Conclusion

Parental drug use had exacted a heavy toll on these children and young people's lives. Those of them who had been exposed to it from an early age, particularly if there had not been another protective adult in the shape of a non-drug-using parent or relative, seem to have found the world a confusing, unreliable, frightening and lonely place. When drugs came first, the children would take a lesser place, and their needs would largely be ignored or go unnoticed. This would leave them vulnerable to harm in the shape of neglect of their material, medical and physical needs. The hidden harm however lay in the costs to their emotional and social development through their perception that they were not as important as their parents' drugs were. It was this that those children and young people who could find the words really articulated. The important point is that these children, whilst dependent on their parents, were also damaged by them. The very people to whom they looked for care, for certainty and security in their developmental journey through childhood, were often those least able to provide it. The world they learned about through their parental relationships was not a safe, benign place. It could be unpredictable, was often dangerous and frightening and it was difficult to know whom to trust.

The experience of such adversity in the earliest years will have forever marked most of these children, although to varying extent. That some manage to find a way through it to become healthy adults is testimony to the amazing resiliency of some children. However, the available research indicates that many have difficulties in adolescent and early adulthood (Clark *et al.* 2004 2005) and not the least of these is the likelihood that they will go on to use drugs problematically themselves. This subject is addressed in Chapter 8: Proliferating Problems: Exposure to Drugs and Drug Initiation, which considers the elevated likelihood that children of drug-misusing parents and siblings of problem drug users will develop problems with drugs.

Chapter 7

Stepping into the Breach: When the Extended Family Takes on the Care of Children

It's a shame, it's the weans that suffer. It's the weans that suffer all the time.

(Grandparent: Mrs Lennie)

Introduction

The extended family has long stepped into the breach where families have got into difficulties; indeed there is a social expectation that relatives should be the first port of call where help or support is needed. In families where drugs are an issue, the assistance offered by the family can very often be critical in protecting and nurturing children through the bad times. The problem, though, is that where drug problems are concerned, the bad times can be long lasting, sometimes permanent, leaving the extended family fully at the helm. Their continued intervention is often all that stands between the child and the care system.

This chapter looks at the role of the extended family, predominantly grandparents, in caring for children with parents with drug problems. The research with 62 parents with drug problems indicated the substantial role taken by the extended family in caring for children. These parents were specifically recruited to this study on the basis that they were actively parenting at least one child: yet of these over half were dependent on high levels of childcare from the extended family, and in a fifth of families one or more children were in the full time care of their grandparents or aunts/uncles. Indeed, where a parent did not have the extended family to fall back upon, it was almost certain that at least one of their children would have been looked after and accommodated at some stage (Barnard 2003). It was this finding that prompted the subsequent set of 20 interviews with grandparents and one aunt, which aimed to explore with them their experience of 'unplanned parenthood' (Minkler, Roe and Roe 1993). Most of the relative carers who were interviewed for this study were in contact with social work. This means that there is less representation of those relative carers who have informally taken on children, although it might be added that the routes to social work these carers had taken were not straightforward and for many the assumption of a parenting role had been an incremental process from initially taking on the care of children informally to seeking, over time, to formalize it.

These grandparents and other relative carers were unequivocal as to the importance of having taken on the care of children. Even so, they acknowledged that there were costs, whether emotional, social, financial or health wise and, in different measure, everyone in the family was affected by it. The chapter begins with a consideration of the continuum of care that was being provided by the extended family as reported by parents and relative carers, before moving on to consider the effects that this had on them all.

When the family steps in

It is worth beginning with an extract from an interview in which a grandparent describes her involvement with her daughter's household and grandchildren prior to the development of a drug problem.

> Even before the drug situation I knew they were tight for money and rather than give them money I'd take along messages [shopping] and that would feed them. And I would take that along and we had quite a good relationship and they had a happy home. And if they needed a television I bought them a television and a video to keep the kids amused. I've done my best for them money-wise but the boys used to come along... Because they only stayed up the road and the relationship was very, very good.

> (Grandparent: Gladys)

The pattern of involvement that this grandparent described was unremarkable to her because it was tied to her sense of her role as a mother and grandparent to support and offer help to her family where she could. So when her daughter began to use drugs, whilst obviously alarmed and distressed, her impulse was to step up this involvement to try to resolve her child's drug problem, and at the same time ensure that the grandchildren's needs continued to be met. This translated into greater oversight, spending more time at the house, taking a greater role in caring for children in feeding and clothing them, taking them to school etc. In essence, in the early days at least, it was an extension rather than a quantum leap on from the kinds of support they expected to be providing to their child's family. Something of this escalating involvement can be heard from the following grandparent:

> I knew there was something wrong but I just couldn't put my finger on it. My brother went up to visit my daughter one time and he seen needles so then I started going up all the time and my daughter would stay in the bedroom with her partner and I noticed then that my grandson wasn't properly looked after. He wasn't up and dressed and out and about and if I did see them out the kids were, well at that time she only had one child … I mean he was clean and things but he just seemed lost and living on crisps and biscuits and things like that so I noticed it and I didn't know what to do. I think I actually spoke to social workers saying that I was a bit concerned, so by then she had a social worker appointed to them and they helped her to get the kids to nursery and different things.
>
> (Grandparent: Pearl)

And for some problem drug using parents this oversight and support might be enough to help maintain their household with some degree of stability. However, as is clear from the following problem drug-using parent's account, it was always a precarious balance because of the instability inherent in the lifestyle associated with the drug use:

> I: What were things like when you stayed in your own house with Layla [daughter]?
>
> R: Not very good, they weren't very good. I mean there would be times where if I had plenty of drugs, or I was like on a period where I was controlling drugs that I would be acting normal, but they wouldn't last very long.
>
> I: How long do you think they'd last?
>
> R: A couple of weeks and then it would make me go back. I would go on the ran-dan [drug rampage] and my ma would see it…my ma made sure I always had contact with her so she would see…and she would take that responsibility away from me because ultimately she was concerned about Layla.
>
> (Problem drug-user parent: Gill)

Many of the parents described a frequent to and fro between their relatives' houses and their own, sometimes staying there for long periods of time with the child and sometimes using it as a place to leave the child whilst they followed the paths their drug use would lead them down, perhaps for weeks or months at a time:

> I just phoned ma mum and I said 'Could you pick David [her son] up from school tomorrow and I'll phone you at the weekend'...but my mum, my dad and David didn't see me for three months from that phone call you know.
>
> (Problem drug-user parent: Kim)

This level of incipient instability was highly disruptive and disturbing to children, but also to the relatives who might be left solely responsible for the care of children. Often at short notice they might have to drop everything to step in:

> She [Jenna: child's mother] was turning up late at the nursery. Haley would be in that nursery at five at night when she should have been out of there about half three, quarter to four...and people phoning me up at [work]... 'Jenna's not came for Haley yet and it's five to five, what are we going to do?' and I'm in my work and I'm like that... 'God's sake, man', I...know like...pure...you're totally stressed out, you know.
>
> (Grandparent: Mrs Blackie)

The flip side, however, was those other times where the child was with the problem drug-using parents and they would be apprehensive as to their grandchild's safety and welfare:

> And there again I was keeping Mia for sometimes a week, weekends, so many days and then I always gave her back. And that poor child...now that it's all coming out. I was putting her back and she was in terrible danger. And I'm so angry at myself for letting it go for so long.
>
> (Grandparent: Mrs Cairns)

The accounts provided by the problem drug-using parents as well as those of the grandparents gave a strong sense of a watchful guardianship to closely monitor the situation for signs that the drug problem was impinging on the care of the children. Some parents acknowledged that it was this watchfulness that tempered their behaviour:

> If I didn't have my mum and dad there, aye, Lucy would probably know a lot more, or I would probably, I would've maybe been doing a lot more in front of Lucy if my mum and dad weren't so involved in my life.
>
> (Problem drug-user parent: Caroline)

Witnessing the diminishing capacity of the parents to cope with their children led to taking the step to have the children on a more permanent basis:

> Most of the time I had him because she was away wandering looking for drugs and she wasn't turning up with money and all the money was getting used for drugs, as you know. So I decided; 'I'm keeping him Meg. I'm not letting you keep him.'
>
> (Grandparent: Esme)

As the following grandparent describes, it was when the third child entered the frame that things began to go seriously wrong in her son's household:

> They were using but not too severe. There wasn't that much abuse at the time that we really would have took much notice of. They coped with it and they were looking after the kids and things like that at that time. It wasn't until Jessica was born that the drugs really got out of hand...
>
> (Grandparent: Mrs Lennie)

It was at this point that their level of involvement shifted into a quite different gear, leading soon after to these grandparents, with the agreement of their son, taking the children. What finally clinched it for Mrs Lennie was seeing the environment within which her grandchildren were living:

> But my two sisters and I went down one day and I was so mortified with the place. I wouldn't let a pig live in it. My sisters and I just lifted black bags and threw every single thing that was in the house out. Their clothes were covered in maggots and the food... They had been bringing sandwiches back from the food kitchen and they were all lying in bags and they were all full of maggots and this is what these weans were living in. The cupboards were all full of syringes so we just threw everything out. That is when I took the weans away.
>
> (Grandparent: Mrs Lennie)

For most of these relatives it was a particular event that finally tipped the balance. Mostly these were events that convinced the grandparent, or in this case the aunt, that the children were unsafe where they were:

> One day I went down when Grace was about six months old. I walked in and there were drug dealers there because she [sister] owed money and they were actually saying to her that they were going to hold the baby over the window because she owed them money. She lived in the high flats then. One of the other times I went up, it was on a Saturday one

weekend. I popped up unexpectedly and there was a strange guy in with Grace and he was sitting feeding her. When I asked where my sister was he said that she was away on a message [shopping]. I mean I didn't know him or anything so I just got the wean ready and took her.

(Aunt: Natalie)

Social work intervention had led to the placement of children in about half of these cases. Social workers did not always initiate these proceedings; it could as easily happen that the relative carer would make contact with social work to alert them to the situation and also to try to elicit their support, not often successfully or, often, to their minds, very effectively. The most likely reason for intervention was concern that the child was at risk through parental preoccupation with drugs, as in the following case:

She [daughter] went out one day with Dylan [baby son] and she came in and she was blootered [incapacitated by drugs]. She couldn't even talk... So she came in and she just sat on the chair and out. We couldn't waken her up... I went 'Oh the wean is due a feed' and unwrapped the wean and he had a bruise mark from the thigh down to there. It was all blue as if the blood had stopped. So I phoned stand-by social work and I told them I was taking the wean straight to Yorkhill [hospital]. They took Dylan in and I came home and I told her to get out. That was it. I was breaking my heart.

(Grandparent: Elspeth)

There were also cases where social work had removed children from their parents as a matter of emergency. The extended family might have to make an immediate decision to take children, knowing that they would be placed in foster or other care if they said no:

One day social work contacted me at work and said...did I know that my youngest grandson had been burnt...I rushed home in a state and I couldn't find my daughter so I phoned social work up and I said to them 'I want these children if they are going into care'...so about half nine that night they brought the two children. So, I had no access to the children's clothes or toys or anything. I couldn't get into her home. I had no keys. The children came with what they stood in.

(Grandparent: Pearl)

Although initially children might be placed with relatives on a temporary basis, on the assumption that the parent could stabilize their drug problem, in practice these placements often stretched to months or years. Mostly there was subsequent, if erratic contact by one or both parents with the children but for two of these families there was no further contact with the children by the mother or father.

> My daughter is a drug addict and an alcoholic. She had Jacob when she was 23. Both of them, Jacob and May, came to live with us when they came out of hospital but May just disappeared and never came back for him, literally never came back for him... Then she went on, later on, to have Joe who is now six. She put him into social work care in November 2001 just for a rest but she never came back for him either... Just disappeared. Went and got on with her drug life.
>
> (Grandmother: Hazel)

The reasons that relatives gave for taking on the care of children were always framed in terms of the children's wellbeing and protection but more importantly it was because these children were part of their family and vulnerable. They loved them and felt a responsibility towards them, and perhaps particularly because of their circumstances, were very protective:

> These wee souls have only got me...they've not got anybody. They've only got me.
>
> (Grandparent: Rosaline)

However, taking on this responsibility carried many costs for relatives, for the children and for their parents. Even whilst it was seen as the right thing to have done, none of those who had taken on the care of their relatives' children did so without struggling at some level; whether, for example, financially, or through ill health, or through the disturbed behaviours that a substantial number of the children reportedly displayed. In this next section, attention turns to these costs, considered in terms of the relatives and the children they had responsibility for.

The consequences of assuming care of children
Adjusting to the changed family situation
Many adjustments needed to be made by everyone in the family to the inevitable disruption brought about by the addition of usually young, and often somewhat traumatized, children to the home of their grandparents or aunts and uncles. Most of these relatives (12/20) had taken on the care of two or three children and, in one case, a grandmother had her daughter's five children living with her permanently. Additional members to the household inevitably put strains on space, time and other resources; all of which could lead to resentment, argument and tension in the house. This can be heard in

the following description of the response of this grandparent's two teenage sons to the addition of their two nephews to their home:

> Oh my God, they were all fighting and carrying on. Ben, he's the oldest, he didn't want them here because he couldn't get his rest and his pals was coming up and all these weans were running about. Logan complained because he lost his room because he's not got a room of his own now... That was the worst part, trying to get them to accept that the children were going to stay here. They were all arguing. Ben didn't want them here. He would say, 'How is it our lives need to get disrupted?'
>
> (Grandparent: Pearl)

The addition of the children to the household diverted attention that could have otherwise been given to other family members, including other grandchildren. The needs of the grandparents' own children could also be somewhat eclipsed by the new household members, particularly if they were very young and necessarily more demanding. The dilemma this could create was soon demonstrated for a grandparent when her son fell into a fire and needed emergency treatment:

> In that moment I thought: what do I do here? If my son is going to be ill, where do my priorities lie, with the two young grandsons, or with my own son?
>
> (Grandparent: Lila)

There were other members of the family who felt strongly that it should not have to come to such a choice; they were angry that the problem drug-using parent in abrogating their responsibility to raise their own children had so burdened the grandparent or aunt:

> A few of them aren't too pleased that me, at my age, is looking after them. I mean, you see Ann [daughter] walking about with her dog and gives us a wave and I'm running up and down to the doctors when one of the boys isn't well.
>
> (Grandparent: Rosaline)

Overlaying this however, was the anger and great upset in the family that the parent was not looking after their own children. It was unfathomable:

> And I loved her to bits and I tried everything. I just couldn't understand how she couldn't get involved with her own two weans you know. Especially with Conor the way he is [with cerebral palsy].
>
> (Grandparent: Esme)

The sense of shame that grandparents felt over their child's inability to parent was a further encumbrance:

> And what I think feels even worse, is because you have the guilt that it's your child that's caused this… It's like because you feel responsible.
>
> (Grandparent: Viv)

The accrued stigma associated with the drug problem particularly concentrated around issues of childcare. It tainted everyone in the family and so was part of the dynamic by which families became socially isolated.

Additional strains were placed on marital relations, particularly in reconstituted families where the grandparent's partner was not directly related and did not necessarily share the same acute sense of family obligation to help the forsaken child:

> If Jenna goes back on the drugs, then Haley [granddaughter] will be took off her by the social workers again, they'll be looking at me to take her and then me and Dan'll not be the 'gether and I'll be on my own looking after Haley, and that's a fact.
>
> (Grandparent: Mrs Blackie)

This grandparent had a strong sense of her obligation to her granddaughter but equally well appreciated its likely costs to her personal relationship with her partner.

The financial implications of taking on the children

Inevitably there were increased financial costs for the household. These were rarely covered by the social care system, even when it was formally recognized that the grandparent or aunt had become the legal carer. These extra costs had to be absorbed by the extended family: no mean feat considering that many were pensioners, already living in straitened circumstances. For many of the relative carers interviewed, the financial implications of taking on the children had not been a big part of their initial calculations, yet it became a perennial source of anxiety as many struggled to meet these extra costs:

> I thought I'd went round all the issues that would be, but the funny thing I never thought on was money…know, 'how am I going to manage?' but all of a sudden it was like I had these two extra to feed on a daily basis, I had to buy them like different things, socks and shoes and school bags…
>
> (Grandparent: Viv)

A number of relative carers had been in employed work prior to assuming the full time care of their grandchildren but had either to reduce or give this up once they had taken on care of the children. This inevitably had an impact on everyone in the household, including, in this case, the aunt's younger son who had also to get used to having less:

> From then we just lived really, really poorly. I mean, I've got a gas meter and an electricity meter but when people came down they said the house was freezing. To us it was just... If we were cold we would put jumpers on and things like that. And my shopping... We never went without, but it was just cheaper brands. We had to cut corners some way. I mean there was no McDonalds and no just jumping to the pictures [cinema]. For the last three years that's the way it's been. Having to watch every penny.
>
> (Aunt: Natalie)

For some, the additional costs of having the children could not be absorbed within their already meagre incomes, which could mean having to go into debt. This was not only a further source of worry; it was also humiliating to those who had never previously had been in debt, nor publicly had to go cap in hand:

> I ended up in rent arrears. I always kept plenty of food for the kids. I bought them clothes. I had to buy prams. I thought, something's got to give and if it means my rent, then, so be it. I can't say, 'well, I won't buy food for them', that would have been crazy, or clothes, they would have been back in care. So, I thought, 'they are not doing without. Why should they? I'll give them everything they need, the rent can remain unpaid and if it goes to court, I'll tell them why', which I did...but it was the embarrassment... I'd never been in court. I'd never been in trouble.
>
> (Grandparent: Edith)

Many of the grandparents had at first been reluctant to have contact with any agency; some felt it took away their control over the situation. Probably relatedly, other carers did not want official agencies prying into their family circumstances, still others were troubled by the possible interpretation that they were in it for the money they could prise out of social services:

> As I says to [social worker] the reason why I don't ask them for anything is that I don't want them thinking that I've only got these weans to get money off the social work. That's not why I've got these weans, I've got these weans because I want to have them. They're my grand weans and I'd rather have them than see some stranger with them. But as [social

worker] says, 'That's not the point, they should be helping you. They should have helped you long before now.'

(Grandparent: Mrs Lennie)

It was also the case that some relative carers, when they assumed care of the children, did not ask the parent to transfer over to them the state-paid child benefit allowance. The grandmother in the following case had made this decision deliberately in the early years because she felt it was bad enough that she was taking the children, although remarkably so, given that she took on the costs of bringing up her daughter's five children:

So, when I got it fixed with the social worker she [daughter] wouldn't give me the money. She still gets their money. It's still in her name but I've accepted that. I mean, she gives me it now. I've got the cards and that for the child benefit and her social money. I get that now. I feed them, I buy them clothes. I never ever took it off her before because I felt that was taking the weans away. I never ever wanted to take them away from their mother as such.

(Grandparent: Edith)

Other grandparents reported that at first they had not known that any state payment could be transferred to them once they assumed care formally and had not claimed for financial assistance until much later on.

Coping with the children

Oh it's an awful life; it's a shame for these kids. There's a generation is lost and there's going to be a generation coming up that's going to be lost. Because how are they going to get rid of all the anger?

(Grandparent: Gladys)

By far the biggest challenges for these families lay in the troubled behaviours of many of the children they had taken on. In 11/20 families one or more of the children had behavioural problems that had required psychological intervention or had serious behaviour problems at school and with peers, three had developed alcohol and drug problems and a further two were self-harming. Many of these children had been exposed to traumatic events through the lifestyle associated with their parents' drug problems. In seven families the children had lost either one or both of their parents to a drug overdose; in two families the children had been present at these deaths; one child had witnessed the vicious attempted murder of her mother; two children's mothers were in psychiatric units and one father of a four-year-old boy was severely ill with Hepatitis C. Inevitably this level of exposure to trauma greatly affected these children. They also struggled with a deep-seated sense of loss and insecurity, sadness and anger stemming from feelings of abandonment by their parents.

At the beginning, when children first came to live with their grandparent or aunt they were reported to have great trouble adjusting to routines, as most were not accustomed to regular bedtimes or mealtimes but had apparently lived a chaotic life:

> But then when we first got her, the behaviour was just so impossible. She would…she doesn't sleep, I mean we've got her into a sleeping pattern now where she'll even ask to go to her bed if she's up past her bed-time, mealtimes just a disaster, she won't eat. I think it's because she wasn't getting meals put down to her at a certain time, or maybe her feeding was so erratic that she wasn't…she was getting whenever she opened her eyes in the morning, if she was hungry she was getting a sweet instead of getting a breakfast, or cereal or whatever.

> (Grandparent: Sonya)

Most felt they had been successful, after a time, in instituting routines with the children. Adding some consistency into their lives was seen as having helped considerably in managing the household and in maintaining the children on an even keel. However it was the children's contact with the parent that was most likely to upset the applecart. The best outcome was where parental contact with the children was regular and consistent; where it was erratic and uncertain, where promises were made and broken, was the worst.

> Sometimes she was granted access but she didn't turn up. They would be standing with their faces at the window waiting for her, so they were disappointed, but that happened so many times that I had to pick up the pieces and explain, you know, that maybe something had turned up, or maybe she got the days mixed up.

> (Grandparent: Pearl)

Such events had a knock on effect on the children's behaviours, derailing the stability of the household and leading to an increase in problems played out at home. Parental visits were often described as disruptive and unsettling for everyone concerned:

When the mother comes on the scene they two get agitated and start fighting and shouting and bawling and what not… Life is a hell and you're left to pick up all the pieces because she'll be in their life again.

(Grandparent: Gladys)

The impression gained from these interviews was of very unpredictable patterns of parental contact with children. In the following case the contact was intermittent, but could be measured in weeks, however in some other cases there might not be parental contact for months, or even years:

I: How often do they [parents] see Audrey?

R1: Och they've not seen the wean…she's not turned up for a visit… Once, last week, on the wean's birthday, was the first time for about four weeks, she just keeps on missing…

R2: She misses all the visits.

(Grandparents: Gavin and Frances)

The interviews with problem drug-using parents confirmed the likelihood of erratic patterns of contact with their children. Although it was clear that the key problem was just how unpredictable their lives were, there were other issues too. Parents described guilt and sadness at having given up the children and the trauma of leaving children who would often become distraught at the end of the visit. All of these factors were part of the following problem drug-using parent's description of her reduced contact with her children when they were living with her sister:

Even when I was out using and that, I could see them anytime. It was just that I didn't bother and the fact because I didn't have any money to take them out you know I felt guilty going up to see them…and I didn't want to have to take them back and leave them there so I just didn't go at all.

(Problem drug-user parent: Sian)

A further factor that probably affected the parent's contact with children was the angry or cold reception they might receive when they did appear in the family home because of their drug use and its effects on all their lives. Also, pre-existing and unresolved family difficulties would be part of the dynamic and would find a focus in the parent's drug-related behaviours so that conflict would be very likely when they visited. Whatever the problem drug-using parent's rationale for infrequent visits, however, their children found it hard to live with the disappointment:

> It all came out when she [15-year-old niece] had been drinking. She felt that she wasn't loved by her mum and dad. She feels that she wasn't loved.
>
> (Aunt: Natalie)

The simple fact was that as much as the children loved their grandparents or aunts, etc., they wanted parents who were there for them:

> Brandon…used to break his heart. The other night there in fact…he takes wee notions for his mammy and he breaks down and he cries 'Mum, Mum'.
>
> (Grandparent: Bea)

The hurt that children felt would turn to anger that was played out in the home and was often directed at the grandparents. Coping with the distress of the children in their care presented significant difficulties for the aunt and grandparents interviewed. They struggled to contain and ameliorate the children's anger and sadness and tried hard to compensate for the disappointments of not having their parents in their lives. They understood the provenance of the children's anger, but it was still hard to accept when it was being directed at them:

> When she's hurting, it's hurting us as well and we get to the point where we can't help her. We think 'what else can we do for her?' But we don't know what to do. She's hurting, she's angry at her mum, she's angry at…she takes it out on us because we're closest to her.
>
> (Grandmother: Sonya)

Similarly, this grandma perceived that her eight-year-old grandson's anger and resentment at having to live with her stemmed from his sense of abandonment by his mother:

> He's always been a hyperactive difficult child but, 'em…when he found out last year (that his mother had a drug problem)…we were coming down that road, 'you fucking bastard, you bitch, I hate you', that's what I get when he goes into these moods…and then last week he was really bad… 'I hate you, I hate you, I don't want to live here, you're nothing but a fucking old fogey, I don't want you to come to the school to get me.'
>
> (Grandparent: Mrs Leeson)

Mostly these were not behaviours that were contained in the home, but spilled into other areas of the children's lives, at school and in their relations with peers:

> He's got problems at school 'cause he won't do what he's told at school, and on the bus going to school there's a problem there as well with it because he's just hitting other children on the bus and things like that you know. He's not an easy wee boy to bring up...
>
> (Grandparent: Josie)

Those relatives caring for children whose patterns of behaviour were troubling, described bewilderment as to how to best respond, particularly as the children got older and more physically assertive. Two of these grandparents described feeling increasingly powerless to influence their grandsons and were somewhat intimidated by them too:

> R: They just won't do anything that I tell them to do. I'm losing my control, I'm losing control in the older they're getting and it's not a good feeling.
>
> I: It must be a bit frightening in a way as well?
>
> R: It is frightening. My daughters are frightened. They say 'They're acting like that the now, what like are they going to be when they're 16/17? They'll maybe start attacking you.' I said 'I'd jail them, I would jail them.' But you just take it day by day.
>
> (Grandparent: Gladys)

Grandparents expressed a kaleidoscope of emotions that indicated their sense of the enormity of what they had taken on; it had been for the best and often the *only* thing they felt they could do in the circumstances but this was also more than tinged by uncertainty and anxiety as to how things would turn out. There was little doubt that, in a different world, the children would have been better raised by one or both of their parents and saved the burden of hurt through rejection and loss. For a minority of relative carers, this translated into an uncertainty as to whether they had done the right thing by taking the children from the parent in the first place. What if they had not stepped in? Would the parent have faced up to his or her childcare responsibilities better and come off the drugs? Would it have saved this grandmother's daughter from her eventual overdose and death?

Sometimes I look back and think I wish I had put him into care to give her a fright. She might have came off them; we might still have had her.

(Grandparent: Myra)

A few of the problem drug-using parents themselves echoed this question, and in at least one case, the refusal of the grandfather to take the child, which in turn led to his placement in foster care, had been the spur to the mother's stabilisation on methadone (Barnard 2003). However, putting into practice the idea of placing a child in care in the hope that it would motivate the parent to come off drugs ran counter to the prime aim of most of these grandparents to keep their grandchildren safe, and this to their minds was best achieved by keeping them in the family.

The costs of parenting a second time around

I never ever thought I'd see myself at my age with two young weans.

(Grandparent: Bea)

Taking on parenthood a second time took its toll on the grandparents, even whilst such close contact with their grandchildren also brought many pleasures. The sheer amount of additional housework was tiring; the grandchildren needed attention and they wanted to be played with too:

And everything is more of an effort now. Maybe it's my age, I don't know. He even says to me 'You're no fun anymore.' And I try to explain, 'Alasdair I'm getting older and I don't really feel like running about.' I mean he wants me to go out and play football and stuff like that you know?

(Grandparent: Myra)

Meeting the needs of the grandchildren and any others in the house was described as taking up virtually all the day leaving them with little time that was just for them:

You've not got a life, you've not got a life of your own. There's definitely no life there for you. It's alright if you've even got your husband with you because I would say 'I'll maybe nip out a wee while' and he'd be there to look after them. But when you're on your own you're stuck in the house and whether they're out or not you've got to be here for them coming back. So you've not really got a life.

(Grandparent: Gladys)

This situation will of course chime with most parents, particularly those caring for young children. However, these grandparents had already done all this once before, with their own children. At this stage in their lives many of their peers were free of these responsibilities and could engage more in leisure and social pursuits geared to their own age:

> So my whole day was wrapped around…I didn't feel as if I had a minute to myself. And there's sometimes I would just like to put on my coat and not say 'I've got this responsibility, who'll look after the weans? Who'll put the weans to bed?' I'm not one for going out all the time but I used to like to say 'Oh I'll go over to our Jim's or that.'
>
> (Grandparent: Elspeth)

Another important factor was the ill health of a substantial proportion of these grandparents. Half of the grandparents interviewed reported debilitative health problems such as arthritis and emphysema:

> I mean I'm rotten with arthritis, this hip's bad, this one's worse; I need operations on that. I've got arthritis more or less from my head to my toes and there's days I could scream with the pain, and that's being quite honest with you. But again, what can I do? I've got to think on the kids.
>
> (Grandparent: Edith)

These health problems clearly had an impact on the capacities of the grandparents and raised questions over their long-term ability to cope and inevitably, too, about the future of the children in their care:

> I'm not unhealthy or anything like that but if I fall not well then I make myself really, really ill. I panic if something happens to me and I get myself into a terrible, terrible state. If I get ill what's going to happen to them? Because there is nobody else that I can talk to or turn to, family wise, because every one of my family are all junkies.
>
> (Grandparent: Esme)

This fear of what might happen if the grandparent fell seriously ill was shared by some of the grandchildren and inevitably added to their sense of insecurity:

> I: Do you find yourself thinking what the future is going to be like?
>
> R: Aye and Alasdair does as well. He's got a fear. He keeps saying to me 'Please going to not die in your bed.' So he's obviously thinking that as

well. I'm not young so 'who's going to look after me if she goes.' It's a terrible thing for a wee boy to be thinking.

(Grandparent: Myra)

In both of the above cases the children's mothers had died through drugs. For the other carers there was always the possibility, however small, that things would change, that the parent with the drug problem would find a way out of drugs and might then be in a position to assume at least some of the care of their children:

Well. I think, truthfully, I am beginning to tire. I mean I'm 75. I don't think a woman at 75 should be expected to…and I've had a double mastectomy. I've had my two breasts off, you know, so I'm beginning to feel…over a 23 year period that was since I had the cancer and eight year ago it came back. So, now I'm feeling a wee bit as if I've had enough you know. I truthfully think that I would love my daughter to be able to take her boys back and I think she is getting there.

(Grandparent: Rosaline)

On a day-to-day basis however the relative carers worked on the premise that their situation for the foreseeable future was to look after the children in their care. They had taken on the task of caring for them and they would carry this out for as long as they were able:

They weans are my legal responsibility. I've accepted them legally. I mean she takes them out and that. I mean, I don't want in my head to be saying, 'what's she doing out while I'm stuck in here with the weans?' I don't want that in my head because this is the job I took on. If you take them, what is the use of regretting it? You take them to keep them from being with the drug addict so why worry if the drug addict disappears and doesn't take responsibility?

(Grandparent: Lila)

Perhaps this grandparent was unusual for her determination not to feel resentful, however, she shared with the other relative carers an acceptance of her responsibility and with it the will to find a way through, even despite the difficulties such responsibility almost always brought in its wake.

Conclusion

The numbers of extended family members who have taken on the care of children because of their parent's drug problem might evade precise quantification but all the signs are that their contribution is substantial and significant. Families step in because they are all that stands between these children and the care system and they want to keep children in the family. However, in taking this step the extended family has to adjust at many levels. The extra accommodation of one or, frequently, more children puts pressure on space, on finances, on family dynamics and on the health of the main carer. Like informal family carers generally, the costs of taking on this caring role are rarely acknowledged and often ignored, even whilst it is apparent that without their input, the children would have to be accommodated by local authorities, at a cost far greater to the child than could be measured in monetary terms.

Even with the intervention of the extended family, it was apparent that these children struggled with entrenched worries and anxieties that stemmed sometimes from the traumas they had been exposed to through their parents' drug problem and sometimes from their insecurities and fears over their current living situation. When one adds into this equation the children's reportedly profound feelings of rejection and loss, one gets a sense of the enormity of the challenge facing the extended family and their courage to accept it.

One of the great worries expressed by the grandparents was that these children might too fall victim to drugs. Their fears for their welfare stemmed from a sense that the children's emotional vulnerability might lead them into drug problems too. The degree to which proximity to drugs and exposure to their use might influence drug initiation is the subject of the next chapter.

Chapter 8

Proliferating Problems: Exposure to Drugs and Drug Initiation

Introduction

When children's lives are so closely bound up with the drug worlds that their mothers or fathers, sisters or brothers inhabit one has to ask what might be the consequences of this for their own journeys to adulthood? In particular, are such children more likely to develop drug problems themselves? On the basis of what has been presented this far, it would be hard not to anticipate the likelihood of problems at some level. However, the picture is complex and this research whilst at one level confirming the elevated likelihood of developing problems with drugs, also found that there were children who confounded such expectations. Similarly, it would be a narrow vision that focused only on the intergenerational transmission of drug problems; the responses of children to differential adversities seem unlikely candidates for neat categorization. The following chapter unpicks some of these issues through looking at the narratives of siblings and also of children of problem drug-using parents.

The data for this chapter derive from two research projects; interviews with 36 children and young people in the 'Growing up in drug dependent household' study and interviews with 24 siblings with drug problems and 20 siblings in the JRF research 'Drugs in the family' (Barnard 2005a). In this latter study, half of the problem drug-using siblings interviewed reported having a brother or sister with a current or past problem with drugs; in three of these families multiple siblings (three or four) had developed serious drug problems. In the former study a minority (10/36) reported the development of their own drug problems. An important caveat, however, concerns the different average ages between samples; children and young people in the first study were on average 14.8 years (range 8–22 years); in the second study the average age of siblings was 19 years (range 13–23 years). Clearly, age is an issue given that drug problems are most likely to occur from mid-adolescence onwards. Some of the differences in relative uptake of illegal drugs between the two samples will be age related.

This chapter divides into three sections. These consider how routine and deliberate exposure to drugs influenced drug initiation. Exposure to drugs is the most likely precursor to drug initiation, however a distinction is made between routine exposure to drugs on account of them being part of the life of a parent or sibling and deliberate exposure to drugs by a parent or sibling. The literature on initiation of drug use by siblings identifies role modelling and advocacy as potentially influential and this is supported by the findings from this research. The positive modelling of drugs and active encouragement of siblings to initiate drug use is part of the dynamic that leads other siblings into using drugs. None of the children of drug-misusing parents described parents as positively modelling or advocating initiation of drugs such as heroin. The final section considers those siblings of problem drug users as well as the children of problem drug users who turned away from drugs despite their exposure to them.

Routine exposure to drugs

Both routine and deliberate exposure to drugs could (and did) result in drug initiation. Chapter 6 described the exposure of children of drug-misusing parents to the paraphernalia and use of drugs, often many times over. An added dynamic where one or both parents were preoccupied with their own drink or drug problems was that it could also strengthen the negative influences of older siblings and peers (Duncan *et al.* 1996b; Vakalahi 2001). The siblings of problem drug users also commonly reported being exposed to drugs, although usually at a lesser intensity.

> R: Well…see when, eh, my mum was on the drink? She would let all of us in, and my wee sister would be there and there'd be a few users in the house, and all the drunk people. And my mum knew it would be going on, like jagging [injecting] in the bedroom and…she knew Colette [younger sister] was there but she…she just…kept drinking.
>
> I: Kept drinking?
>
> R: Aye, just didn't bother her. She wouldn't allow it when she was sober. D'you know what I mean?
>
> (Problem drug-using sibling: Annette)

Virtually all the problem drug-using siblings reported that their brother or sister had been exposed to their drug use in some degree. At minimum this involved seeing the effects of the drug use on their own behaviour but more usually also involved having seen drugs, the paraphernalia associated with their use and often too having been present whilst drugs were being used. Five of the problem drug-using siblings reported that none of their siblings had seen drugs or drug use, through either their own efforts at secrecy, their exclusion from the family home and/or the strict enforcement of rules restricting use of drugs whilst in the home. However, as with parental drug use, this seemed difficult to sustain:

I: Yeah but have you ever seen her using heroin or anything?

R: Naw, I've never seen it.

I: Do you think she keeps it away from you?

R: She does. But it was a good few years ago before my mum and dad really found out about it. I was staying with my sister and I was just looking through her cupboard and I found a teaspoon all burned at the bottom. That was one thing that made me click on that she was using something…because that was unusual. I've only ever seen that in like drug adverts or something, like burning heroin with a spoon and I was like 'Yeah, wait a minute.' But I kept it to myself, I let it pass so I did.

(Sibling: Andrew)

Some problem drug-using siblings described having used heroin in front of their younger siblings but had tried to pass off the drug as something else, usually as cannabis or cannabis oil:

But see my wee brother at ten…I took him all the time and watched him. I took him for two weeks here and weeks there…I've done it in front of him every day and he knows all about it. I told him it was hash at first and he's like that 'That's not hash, I know what that is. I've seen it on the polis stuff that they bring to school.'

(Problem drug-using sibling: Fiona)

The success of such efforts at subterfuge was obviously dependent on the lack of knowledge of the other sibling, which was clearly not the case for this boy. Sometimes too the will to conceal the drug use was absent:

I: Right, right. So she [younger sister] knows what it [the drugs] was and all that?

R: Aye she knows what it was but again I didn't care because I was needing it and I was taking it. And I wasn't caring, I wouldn't have cared if it was my ma that was sitting there.

(Problem drug-using sibling: Ali)

One sister recounted the point from which she ceased to try and hide her drug use from her younger brother and openly used in front of him. As she herself points out, this came about through not sustaining the care to keep it hidden:

Now, whenever he walked in my room I'd be like [gasps] and I'd hide it or I'd drop it so he never seen it but…I remember he walked into my room one day and I just didn't care. I just sat there like that and I went…I stopped tooting and I looked and went 'what is it?' and he's like…pure…he didn't know what to say. He went 'oh, forget it' and he walked out.

(Problem drug-using sibling: Mandy)

Where younger children were in the care of their older drug-using siblings, they could be exposed to drug use outside of the home too. For instance, this 13-year-old girl revealed how, unbeknown to her mother, at an early age she and her nephew (the son of her drug-using sister) were often taken to houses where drugs were being dealt and used:

I: What kind of things were you seeing?

R: Like I saw Amanda taking drugs, heroin and stuff and I saw her boy-friend.

I: How was she taking it?

R: Injecting it in her arms and she was, em, burning it and smoking it and stuff.

I: Right. And was she trying to hide it from you?

R: No, not…sometimes, sometimes she did.

I: And when was it you were seeing it and where were you?

R: Oh…she used to go out and do it and she took me out one day and she was like going into people's houses and she was leaving me in other rooms, know when I was older, she was leaving me in rooms but I can remember when I was younger she'd do it in like stairwells of people's closes [tenement flats]... And I was like beside her.

(Sibling: Danielle)

Proximity and experimentation

Routine exposure to drugs provides the opportunity for children and siblings to develop a curiosity as to their effects, which might encourage experimentation. There is also the possibility that use of drugs such as heroin might conceivably normalize its use such that societal taboo warnings against heroin use would be rendered ineffective. The interviews with younger siblings indicated that proximity to drugs played a role in encouraging a curiosity that resulted in experimentation and the development of drug dependence. In the case of Annette's young sister Colette, cited above, and also Barry watching his older brother with his friends, there was an interest in what was going on:

> And he used to just sit in and he would be puffing cannabis and maybe taking the odd bit of speed and...well, I used to go in and chap [knock on] the door, curiosity...I'd want to sit in with them but I was never allowed to...the odd time, the odd time he would say 'aye well you can sit in for five minutes,' 'cos I was annoying them that much, and then pap [shut] us out again.

(Problem drug-using sibling: Barry)

When Barry first bought and used heroin it was in the company of friends. However he knew what to do and how to use it from having watched his brother use it for years before him. It was also through watching her brother smoke heroin and being curious as to its effects that Chantelle first used it:

> I: And how much did you know what was going on?

> R: 'Em, quite a lot, he would sit and do it in front of me all the time, I used to sit and say, 'give us a smoke, give us a smoke' and one time he did...and I was sick!

(Problem drug-using sibling: Chantelle)

This curiosity was also present in the children of problem drug-using parents, as is illustrated by the following young person, who even despite hating the associated behaviour, wondered what it was about drugs that motivated them to use them:

> I don't know, it sounds a bit wrong because I hated smack, I hated it, I just hated the stuff, I hated the people and if they came in the house I'd be like 'fucking smack head', I hated them and I wouldn't go out with them and then like one night I just thought I wonder what it's like to run…a line of heroin.
>
> (Child of problem drug-using parent: Karen)

Many of the siblings, whether drug using or not, spoke of their expectation that their elder sibling was someone to look up to and be an example to them. When these elder siblings went on to use drugs problematically there were those younger siblings who modelled these behaviours. Chantelle explicitly acknowledged this, as did other of the interviewed siblings. It would not necessarily be the older sibling who actually initiated the drug use, this could happen with peers. However, being consistently exposed to drugs and drug taking might work at an insidious level to demystify drug use, to teach its use and through proximity make possible casual experimentation without fully understanding the possible personal consequences of such an action. Those children of problem drug-using parents who developed drug problems in adolescence described a learned sense of the mundaneity of drug exposure and use:

> I didn't know if it was right or if it was wrong, I didn't know it was wrong, know what I mean, I just…I thought it was something normal that you would do at that time.
>
> (Child of problem drug-using parent: Angela)

For two of those young people with drug problems, part of their learning about drugs was the role they understood that drugs played for their parents in dealing with the world and as a response to stress:

> I: You know you started using through your pals bringing drugs in, do you think that that was the only reason or do you think…
>
> R: No, as I say, I thought anybody in my family had a problem, they disappeared into the kitchen for a bit a tinfoil. So I had a problem, so I tried it.
>
> (Child of problem drug-using parent: Madison)

Routine exposure to parental drug use had been instrumental to the first use of drugs for 8/10 young people who had become seriously drug involved, because drugs were easily available and, through observation, they learned how to use them. The following account relates to a time when Donna was eight years old:

I weren't taught what was right and what was wrong and at anytime, there was like ten of us living there and there was only me, Mum and my dad that was family, the rest were all lodgers and most of them…were buying the gear [drugs] off of her and they were just all off their head all the time. So there were people crashed out on the sofa and [I'd] go in there and they'd leave lines [of cocaine] on the table, I know it's madness 'cause it can get blown off, but I would just go in there and snort it all or lick it…

(Child of problem drug-using parent: Donna)

The following section on deliberate exposure relates only to those young people whose brothers and/or sisters had developed drug problems. As previously mentioned, none of the children of problem drug-using parents described having been deliberately initiated into drugs by parents. However, it was the case that once a child's drug habit was formed, their parents apparently accommodated, adapted and utilized it, as demonstrated in the following interview extracts:

I first started using…I'd just gone 11, two days after me eleventh birthday…injecting about 12…when me dad found out it, it freaked him out and he was like; 'I'll buy you as many bags as you want just as long as you toot it' so that's what I did and like she'd [her mother] come home and I'd just do it in front of her and it just wouldn't bother her one bit and like at first I'd be funny and like I'd go in the bathroom and you know not do it in front of her and then she'd be like 'I'm not bothered', she went 'well, I am bothered 'cause you're my daughter, you know what I mean, doing something like that in front of me', she says 'but at the end of the day, your dad's paying for it, it's better than you injecting, I'd rather you do ought [anything] than inject'. I just did it in front of her then.

(Child of problem drug-using parent: Karen)

Some of the parent's accommodation of their child's drug problem appeared less motivated by harm reduction than by opportunism. This might take the form of the parent and child teaming up to jointly fund and find drugs or a more explicit use of their child's capital to meet their own drug needs. This was reportedly the case in the following account where a young woman first told her father about her drug use:

I says 'you know I've been using don't you'… And he says 'well stop taking it', I says 'no, it's too late for that, I've already got a habit'…and he went… Phew, I still can't get over this one to this day either, he says 'have you got anything on you' and I says 'aye, how'? And he says 'well give us a wee square up [give him some drugs] and we'll talk about it later'... And we've still never had that talk to this day... And because I gave in that day, my da's always relied on me because I give in to him all the time, I give in to everybody.

(Child of problem drug-using parent: Chloe)

Deliberate exposure

This section considers those accounts in which drugs (or their effects) were deliberately shown to siblings and, in four cases, their use was deliberately advocated. The motives for deliberate exposure were not solely about encouraging use. Indeed, in a number of cases, it was intended to have the opposite effect on the likelihood that a sibling would experiment with drugs such as heroin.

Perhaps the starkest example of a sibling advocating drug use can be found in the following interview excerpt. This problem drug-using sister related how she was responsible for inducting two of her nine siblings into heroin use on the basis that it was an improvement on the substances they were already using:

R: I kind of got my brothers into smack, but anything else they got theirselves into. I think it was me that got them into the smack...

I: OK, so there's three of you. How did you get them into it?

R: Well I didn't get them into it, just kind of introduced them to it. If they were coming down to my house I was giving them a...charge [dose], it just ended up with a habit...

I: So which one was it that got into it first?

R: Em, my older brother. I got him into it first.

I: How did that happen, do you remember?

R: He was on the glue and I used to say to him 'fling the glue bag away and I'll give you a shot of this'. Just used to, like get him to fling his glue bag away and I'd give him a charge and then he just ended up in about it.

(Problem drug-using sibling: Lynette)

It needs to be added that, by her account, Lynette's family had a number of serious problems, particularly severe alcohol dependence on the part of the mother and the numerous partners who had separately fathered each of the nine children. The other reported cases where siblings were introduced to drugs by their siblings were less overtly bleak, couched within frameworks of self-interest or even the sibling's protection.

In the following case, Richard described how his elder brother introduced him to drugs, reportedly to compromise him. Admiration of his elder sibling was part of Richard's explanation for his initiation into heroin; 'If my big brother done it. I would do it.' However, he also considered that his elder brother's self-interest was part of the explanation for his initiation into heroin use, as he made clear in the following narrative account. When Richard threatened to tell his mother that he had found his elder brother using drugs, he claimed his brother had responded by tricking him into using heroin, which therefore implicated Richard in the act.

> I used to blackmail him stupid… So I was like 'I'm going to tell her that'. And he jumped and he's like that, 'going to not tell her, going to not tell her', he's like that, 'look, try it, it's hash oils'. He gave me two lines and I started being sick all over the place. 'How do I get this away?' and he's like that, 'you need to take more' and he was giving me more and I'm whiteying [passing out] all over the place, so…this was eh…just before I was 16 and I hated it. I says 'I'm not taking it any more, I don't want any' and he went 'you tell my ma that I took it, I'll tell my ma that you took it'.
>
> (Problem drug-using sibling: Richard)

A non-drug-using sibling described a situation where her sister had offered her heroin, which to her mind was motivated by the desire to create parity between them where usually there was hostility and rivalry for the mother's attention:

> A couple of times she offered me it… Tara would have loved for me to have turned round and says 'aye' because the whole…she would've went right back and told my mum and dad like that, she'd have loved it just to have one up on me… Sort of to say to my mum and dad 'well no, she's not any better than me', but she never got that chance.
>
> (Sibling: Marie Louise)

Self-interest was also what motivated one drug-using sibling directly to expose his sister to drugs. As he could not go safely to the particular area where the drug dealer lived, he had used her to buy them for him. Unbeknown to him, she started to sample his heroin and developed a drug problem herself.

> I ended up blaming myself for her to start using because…I couldn't go to a certain bit and I used to get her boyfriend to go and score for me and she'd go with him and bring it back to me so I think I might have intro-

duced it d'you know what I mean? Getting her to go and score for me... Then one time I walked in and I caught her with tin foil... Then I knew. But I wasn't really bothered and all that because I couldn't criticize her if I'm using. I was injecting it and she was only smoking it.

(Problem drug-using sibling: William)

Perhaps the most unexpected rationale for deliberate exposure of drugs to other siblings was that it would be preventive. In the following account, a drug-using sibling describes how she tried to encourage her brother to take heroin with her so as to pre-empt any use elsewhere. In retrospect she herself found her reasoning to be bizarre and put it down to the fact that she was greatly under the influence of drugs herself at the time:

I turned round to Nick and I went 'listen, you know what that is don't you?' and he went 'aye, it's smack' like that and I went...I went 'Nick, son, promise me you will never, ever go on that'... But I said to him 'but Nick, what if one of your pals ever offer you it? Curiosity does kill the cat, you know?' and I was like... 'So like, would you say no to your pal?' and he went 'none of my pals touch it'... And I says 'look' and I say – and I can't believe I actually done this. I says 'look, do you want to try it the now so that you've tried it and then you can say "well at least I've tried it and I don't want to go near it"?' and he went 'no' and I went, 'are you sure now cos you can just have... I'll show you what to do...go, just have a wee shot and I'll...then that way, you've tried it.' And I'm saying 'I'll do it for you and then that way you've tried it and you'll see what it's like and you won't, and then you'll not need to try it again.' ... And see when I think about it, thank God he never tried it because it's good, and he'd have thought, 'oh brilliant!' and he'd have kidded on to me, 'that's rubbish, I don't like that' but really inside he'd have been like 'wow, this is amazing!' and he might have ran out the next day to get some. So thank God.

(Problem drug-using sibling: Mandy)

By any account this is an unusual means of trying to prevent drug use. However many of the siblings with drug problems reported drawing deliberately on their experiences of drug dependency to try to discourage their brothers and sisters from using drugs themselves. This ranged from showing drug-related injuries to describing the effects of drugs:

But I've showed her my hole in my groin and I've said 'do you want to end up like that?' I can honestly say that I've got my wee brother and sister terrified of smack. The only way they would take smack is because

I've been that open with them, I've writ them letters, as in I've treated them like adults.

(Problem drug-using sibling: Richard)

It is interesting to note that Richard's account shows both an awareness of the preventive role of exposure and its flip side: that in being open about his drug use, he might also have created an attraction to them.

The sibling's reactions to these prevention activities were rather mixed. Many resented their problem drug-using sibling taking on the role of teacher given these were lessons they themselves seemed unable to heed:

R: I just can't get my mind round how he wants to do it... But then like he would say to me 'never do it' and then like I'd say 'why do you do it?' and he just doesn't answer you.

I: Yeah. And does that annoy you?

R: Aye, like he would tell me, he'd tell me off, but he does it.

(Sibling: Eleanor)

Indeed the following sister makes clear that such advice was entirely counterbalanced by the lessons she drew from her brother's behaviour rather than his words to the contrary:

'Cos like my brother never, ever gave me it or anything or like the guy that I was seeing never, ever gave me it. They just says like 'don't take it' but at the end of the day they were sitting taking it in front of me so... I was like, well, if they can take it how can I not take it? Know what I mean, it can't be that bad. It's like if somebody smokes and they're sitting smoking a fag and they go 'don't smoke'...'uh uh'. 'It's bad for you, just learn from my mistake' and you're like, 'mm, right, well...' I just, I think that's rubbish, somebody saying that to you. I mean like 'don't smoke' and they're sitting with a fag... It's contradicting yourself really isn't it? But that's what they were doing so I tried it myself.

(Sibling: Martina)

Situations where siblings are deliberately offered drugs by brothers or sisters, often in the context of the home environment, have to be seen as posing a high risk of encouraging drug initiation, as drugs are made freely available by trusted familiars. That such exposure would occasion the refusal of drugs is as important as those circumstances within which they are accepted. The following and final section considers the rationales for non-use of drugs that were offered by siblings and children of problem drug-using parents alike.

Turning away from drugs

It is as important to consider the reasons why young people living in intimate proximity to drugs turn away from them as it is to think about their vulnerability to drug initiation. This is underlined by the fact that most of the children and young people interviewed for both of the research projects reported here, did not, at least at that time, go on to develop drug problems.

The didactic role adopted by some parents and siblings in counselling against drugs was not as influential as learning from the example and experience of living with their problem drug-using relative. These children and young people looked at the appearance and behaviours of their relatives and took these as good reasons for not becoming involved in drugs:

> All you need to do is to look at the boy for an example and just see how he's fucked his own life up through drugs and how he's fucked his body up and how he's...he was a big boy know...now he's just a wee skinny, scraggy wee junkie. Sells the Big Issue and that, know what I mean.
>
> (Sibling: Stuart)

It was also their sense of the devastating impact that the drug use had on the family, particularly on their mothers, that affirmed their intention never to become involved in drugs:

> I: That's the worst thing about it [drug use] for you?
>
> R: Ruin your life...and you lose all your family. I seen what it done to Richard, he lost a lot of his family when he was on drugs. Nobody wants to know you. Steal and...everywhere you go, everybody knows you. Just get booed and all that, battered and all that.
>
> (Sibling: Dean)

For children and young people whose parents had drug problems, the impact of living with the effects of drugs on their lives was instructive against entering that lifestyle:

> Never, never in my life, no...no way, after what happened with my mum and dad, no way, nothing, I'd never touch nothing. I know a lot of folk just say that, but from experience, like what's happened; never ever.
>
> (Child of problem drug-using parents: Susan)

There were those who did not think they would ever have become involved in drugs because it was not in their natures. Their exposure to drug use would not, to their minds, alter that situation, although experiencing the impact that it had on the family might have hardened that resolve, as in the case of Martin below:

> I've never…I can honestly put my hand on my heart and say I've never tried any sort of drug, I've never tried smoking a cigarette but just very seldom I would take a drink… I wouldn't say that was because of my brothers, it was just…it's something, it's just something that's never really interested me…
>
> (Sibling: Martin)

Many siblings said they could not understand the attraction of drugs or the associated lifestyle. They saw their brothers or sisters as sad, angry people and considered that it was their drug problems that had largely brought this about. The fact that they could sacrifice so much for drugs was further underlined by witnessing them whilst 'full of it', which state, from their perspective, was neither fun nor sociable:

> I: What, what is your feeling about drugs?
>
> R: That I just wouldn't take them and…I don't understand how like people want to go and do it when you can like get more out of life than sitting about taking drugs.
>
> (Sibling: Eleanor)

Those young people who had witnessed traumatic events like overdoses cited these as powerful reasons not to use drugs themselves:

> Never going to take heroin… After seeing a guy o.d…. Do you know what that means, o.d.?… I just didn't want to know about the stuff… I seen a guy, well, he went into the kitchen and I knew he was taking it… Somebody gave him it and he sat on the couch and he just didn't move or make a sound or anything… And then he just…he wasn't breathing or anything, he was going blue and they phoned an ambulance and the ambulance came and took him away.
>
> (Child of problem drug-using parents: Dan)

These are compelling narratives of how exposure to the effects of drugs deterred experimentation. Yet there was no guarantee that this opposition to drugs would endure. Take for an example the experiences of both Kylie and Shanice below, which were like those of Dan in that they had seen overdose at close quarters, but in both their cases had resulted in the deaths of close family members:

> Three of my uncles have died through drugs... I found my uncle Tom dead on Christmas Day last year with an overdose...and my uncle Jim died three month before, October, with a drugs overdose. It was hard and then, my brother takes it [drugs] so I've grew up with it, grew up with the fact that drugs are in my family and you can't change that but it's a horrible feeling and then I ended up taking it.
>
> (Child of problem drug-using parent: Kylie)

And:

> You would think I would have learned 'cos...my auntie, my dad's sister...died of an overdose. My ma's sister has just came off kit herself. Em...my ma and my da were both on it, so...you would think that would teach you to say 'no', you know what I mean but...
>
> (Problem drug-using sibling: Shanice)

On the basis of these accounts one might feel less than sanguine over the curative powers of experience of the negative effects of problem drug use, even at first hand, to prevent drug involvement.

Conclusion

The reasons why one child develops a drug problem but another does not, appear to evade simple determination. Exposure to drugs and drug use through its close proximity does appear to play an important role in elevating the risk of drug initiation, particularly for siblings of problem drug users. Having an elder brother or sister using drugs in the home can excite the curiosity of a younger sibling and being in a familial relationship can legitimate experimentation and downplay the potential dangers. These same factors might be equally influential for children growing up with parents with drug problems, although their young average age, relative to the siblings, warn against describing any obvious trajectories for their lives.

Teasing out the potential contributory factors and their interaction is an important line of investigation. In particular there is much worth in considering familial and other social factors in terms of how these might enhance children's vulnerability or be protective. The degree of parental supervision and monitoring of the family situation, as well as the quality of the relationships between parent figures and children may be factors contributing to the likelihood of drug use; whether directly through family members or more indirectly through associations with friends engaged in problematic behaviours. The fact that many children resisted such pressures and did not become drug involved is important and is likely to be connected to such dynamics as stability in the home environment over time, close family support (perhaps in the shape of grandparents or aunts and uncles), commitment to conventional social values and having friends not involved with deviant peer networds. For the rest, much may depend on the child's personality and drive to negotiate a safe path away from drugs.

Chapter 9

Practitioner Responses to Drugs in the Home

Introduction

One might expect that the long term and often severe impacts of problem drug use on families would result in a good deal of health and social welfare intervention, particularly where children were concerned. Yet a striking feature of these data was how little intervention there had been, even over many long years of living with the problems created by drugs. In part this will be explained by the nature of the problem: drugs are illegal, problem drug users are stigmatized and parents are afraid of having their children removed. All of these factors encourage secrecy and hiding of problems from public and official notice. In part too, the relative lack of intervention can be explained by the sheer size of the problem and the impossibility of agencies achieving full coverage; 350,000 UK children living with parental drug problems represents a critical challenge for service provision. These are significant factors influencing the situation for children living with parental drug problems. However it is also true to say that, until recently at least, the circumstances of these children have not been deemed sufficiently important to merit specific policy attention (ACMD 2003). Appreciation of the significant numbers of children of problem drug users and raised media attention on a steady increase in significant child abuse cases linked to parental drug use has at last changed the terrain somewhat, whilst at the same time engendering much anxiety as to how best to tread it.

This chapter considers practitioner responses to parenting and child welfare in the context of drug problems. The increased vulnerabilities of these children and the statutory framework around child protection merits a closer consideration of the ways in which practitioners think about such cases. The key question that informs this discussion is why had so few of the children described in this study been the subject of investigation? The interviews with parents, with their children and with grandparents, all indicated a profound level of incipient risk and chronic need, yet there was historically little concomitant evidence of intervention, meaningful or otherwise. Attempting to answer this question requires that attention be paid to the systemic difficulties that agencies have in co-ordinating action given different client bases, agendas and hence priorities, and to anxieties over when it is right to intervene and the consequences of intervention. These are not new problems. Indeed it is the depressing regularity with which these same themes recur in inquiries of non-accidental deaths of children at the hands of their parents or guardians (O'Brien, Hammond and McKinnon 2003; Reder, Duncan and Gray 2003), that underlines both their intractability and the importance of attending to them.

Practitioner responses to the children of problem drug users

This section considers the responses of social workers, health visitors and drug workers to problem drug use in parents and the welfare of children. Obviously the focus groups with practitioners reflected conditions at the time in Glasgow. However the geographical ubiquity of problems across time in recognizing and responding to child welfare difficulties, between and across agencies, is apparent from child welfare research (Buckley 2000; Stevenson 1998). These fault lines were evident in these focus groups. Even despite strategic reconfiguration of services within the city to promote greater co-ordination between services for adults and children, particularly in addiction services, there were still fundamental issues that workers confronted each time they worked with a family. Broadly these concerned the balance between support and surveillance and the process of deciding whether what they saw was neglectful or abusive, and when and how to intervene and to what end. Much as practitioners in these focus groups had apparently taken organizational change on board, and to a large degree were signed up to the principles and practice of joint working, the focus groups strongly indicated fault lines broadly running along the boundaries of professional remit that could and did get in the way of a co-ordinated response to the problems that parental drug use created for family life. The work of this chapter will be to outline these, through paying particular attention to the prime value that these practitioners, in their different ways, accorded the relationships they had with clients.

The primacy of relationships with clients

All of the practitioners emphasized the critical importance of establishing good working relationships with their clients, meaning, most usually, the parents. With such relationships, they felt most confident of being able to do their best for their clients, as well as creating the conditions within which clients could do best for themselves. Cutting across this however, were the tensions created where the agendas and priorities of adult clients did not always dovetail neatly with the needs of their children. Such strains were inevitably present in many of the relationships that practitioners had with problem drug-using parents and presented an ongoing challenge as to their potential resolution (Taylor and Kroll 2004). The difficulty for practitioners was that in addressing divergences between adult behaviour and child interests they risked jeopardizing the relationship that at one and the same time was considered to be the prime vehicle for change.

The kinds of relationships that practitioners establish with their clients inevitably reflect their professional remits. Drug workers in adult-based services were focused on the adult's drug problem, whether in terms of its stabilization, the reduction of drug related harms or moving towards abstinence. Family drug workers were generally concerned with managing parents' drug problems through offering family support and monitoring of the situation for children. Health visitors were concerned with the primary health care, welfare and safety of children under five years of age. Child and family social workers were concerned to support and safeguard the interests of the child. These remits inevitably shaped the practitioner's perspective of the client and their situation and, inevitably too, defined the parameters of the relationship it was possible to establish. Although all of the practitioner groups equally emphasized the value of good working relationships, the key difference between social workers and the other practitioners was that these latter are in voluntary relationships with clients. Without the compliance of the client, neither drug workers nor health visitors have statutory powers invested in their office to insist more forcefully on their client maintaining contact with them. Much therefore rests on the nurturing and guardianship of the relationship, to keep the client engaged with the services offered, so as to most benefit from them. The limits of the voluntary relationship as a vehicle for change were made explicit by one social worker:

> I think what an order [child protection order] would do, would allow the worker to put that wee bit of added pressure on the mother saying, 'Look, we'll expect you to do this and to do that, or to expect you to liaise with us, and if not we have to go back to the [Children's] hearing.' It's easier to do that within an order when sometimes it's more difficult to do it under a voluntary working relationship because you're trying to do it on trust and co-operation, and you've not got the big stick and sometimes it comes down to that.
>
> (Social worker 4: FG6)

Maintaining trust and co-operation with parents whilst at the same time addressing child welfare concerns is a delicate balancing act by any standard. It is at least that bit easier for children and family social workers because child protection is so explicitly their remit; for health visitors and drug workers this remains much more implicit and is overlaid by the framework of offering community support. One gets a sense of the finesse of the balancing trick from the following health visitor's comment:

> That's the other thing, because you always walk a fine line with them because if they find it unacceptable, then you'll not get access to the children at all. That can happen. If you see things are running really badly, then you have to take that risk. But more often than not you're walking that fine line encouraging the person rather than putting more pressure on them.
>
> (Health visitor 1: FG3)

The following health visitor was similarly attentive to the fine balance of interests in describing an approach to a mother whose drug problems were creating concerns for the wellbeing of a baby and also the older child:

> You're trying to make a relationship with her [mother] so that you can maintain contact and some kind of positive relationship with her...and if you address issues too early on she would be off and she would not...and you worry then that you lose the wee boy then, you know you can't offer any support either.
>
> (Health visitor 2: FG9)

Such situations clearly invite caution as a lot is at stake; health visitors spoke of a number of strategies to encourage the parent to reverse the trend, which included using their practice GP to ring the parent, changing health visitor or increasing the number of home visits. In such fashion the relationship might not be jeopardized whilst maintaining a watching brief on the child.

Historically, the highest proportion of referrals to social work come from health visitors (Dingwall and Robinson 1993), which indicates both the breadth of their contact with families in the community and their watchfulness over the welfare of the child. The duality of their role as both supportive and monitoring, although not always comfortable, is part of a learned understanding of what it is to be a health visitor:

> I was once at a conference where a male health visitor stood up and said we should be phoning all our clients in advance, 'after all we're not policemen' and I was sitting thinking that's exactly why society have us because we do...we are proactive, we go out and we work with the

children. A social worker can only get involved if there's been a referral and yes, we have to let people know if the children aren't receiving the basic standards.

(Health visitor 3: FG7)

Until very recently, drug workers have had a specialized remit to act in the therapeutic interests of their adult clients as individuals. The *impact* of their client's drug problem on their children has not previously been integral to that remit. Institutional recognition of the elevated needs and risks confronted by children of parents with drug problems has changed their operational terrain somewhat and brought with it many challenges to working practice (ACMD 2003; Scottish Executive 2003). Central to this has been the push to raise the salience of child welfare in substance misuse work with clients and the inevitable difficulties of overlaying historically quite different service perspectives:

> There is still this kind of two camps, with clients in the middle. There is an awful lot of getting into games with the clients because our perspective is in many ways, is in some cases, different to the perspective to the childcare and you can get the client into denying certain things that they wouldn't necessarily deny if there wasn't a childcare consideration. 'Em we are obviously working on that and hopefully some joint work, the joint posts will be rectifying that.
>
> (Drug worker 2: FG1)

Some of the drug workers clearly struggled with trying to balance their need to create an empathic working relationship with the adult client, with a potentially conflictual insistence upon also maintaining an active and enquiring watchfulness over the children's welfare and wellbeing. Furthermore, it was recognized to be an intrinsic tension:

> You're addiction staff and you do have certain roles and responsibilities which in many ways conflict with childcare. But it's never actually been resolved beyond recognizing that.
>
> (Drug worker 4: FG1)

Drug workers and health visitors alike saw the advantages of not being seen in the same light as social workers by their client groups:

> Addiction workers can sometimes be one of the best people to get information because you're trusted more than the big bad social worker who will take your weans away from you.
>
> (Drug worker 1: FG2)

The juxtaposition of roles is telling. This distancing from the perceived 'policing' role of social workers was commonly emphasized by all of the practitioner groups. Nonetheless, occupying this more trusted position brought with it the difficulties of having to blow the whistle on the parent once it was considered that the adult's behaviour was at odds with the welfare of the child. It was a tension that social workers were acutely aware of:

> You can be a worker for a family and there's going to be an element of conflict between parents' needs and rights and children's needs and rights and that's what it comes down to.
>
> (Social Worker 2: FG8)

One gets a sense that the push and pull between these remits presents a problem to be solved each time such a situation presents itself. Systematic efforts have been made in Glasgow to integrate child welfare into drug and other work with families. However, although good training, supervision and co-location might rectify much, this tension appears fundamental given the prime importance attached to good relationships with clients as a vehicle for access and support. One gets a clear sense of this from the following observation made by one of the health visitors on the difficulties of confronting a situation head on:

> I find that if sometimes maybe you've let things go that you think…because you wanted to maintain that relationship and that's not about letting them off the hook. In a way, it's just keeping the contact flow for the sake of the children at the end of the day.
>
> (Health visitor 1: FG7)

Reticence to lose the purchase afforded by a good relationship with the parent was also voiced by the following drug worker, who like other workers was apparently referring to the situational character of much decision-making in recognizing and responding to problems:

> I mean there are certainly policies about child protection issues, there is training and, there is a notion that we'll all adhere to that, but I think we know that that's not necessarily the case.
>
> (Drug worker 1: FG1)

The degree to which context, including considerations of access and continued engagement, shapes these determinations, rather than the concern or the incident in and of itself has been noted elsewhere (Buckley 2000; Dingwall, Eekelaar and Murray 1983).

For all that social workers were less hostage to the good relationship to gain access to children, they too were very focused on the importance of the relationship they established with the child's parent(s) to change things. For social workers, as any other practitioner, the elevation of the importance of the adult relationship can set up a dangerous myopia where children are concerned.

> And I think if you can actually strike up a relationship where you can communicate and nothing else happens, then I think then you're doing OK.
>
> (Social worker 1: FG6)

These are very lean pickings indeed. The case may perhaps be being over-stated by the social worker making this comment, but establishing a line of communication should not be an end in itself. A relationship 'where you can communicate and *nothing else happens*' offers so denuded a vision of child welfare that one might wonder as to the point of visiting at all? Yet it was not a position arrived through any indifference to the family on the part of the social worker, or, indeed, her supervising senior worker. Rather, it was premised on the notion that any relationship is better than no relationship. This social worker's low expectation of change was borne of many years experience of the intractability of problem drug use and its associated problems and, as can be heard in the following extract, led to the position that just getting in the door was an achievement:

> Sometimes I think, 'God, what's the point in that family, they've been long-term hardened drug-users…' – and I worked with one family for about five years, right? I remember thinking, you know, 'What's happening here? Am I making any impact, is there anything, any point in me going in, really?' And I suppose that was maybe two and a half years down the road, and I think we reviewed it quite regularly and we looked at it and we thought we'd try to break it into stages because I was losing heart for the case…and I remember thinking 'This is just, I'm just going up here and I'm just showing my face and there's nothing getting done.' But see when we looked back and went through supervision and looked through it, at the very, very beginning they would not even answer the door, you know, and then when we were having a big huge meeting to decide their children's future they phoned up and said they couldn't come because they were waiting on their beds being delivered (laughs). You know, things like that, just any avoidance tactic, so look, see when I kind of tracked it, I thought 'My God, I'm actually getting in there and they're talking about their drugs and they were being really open with

me' you know, so that restored my faith a bit, to be honest, because before that I was thinking 'this is hopeless, this is absolutely, I'm just going in here and they're just saying what they think I want to hear.'

(Social worker 1: FG6)

The jointly undertaken effort by the social worker and her senior to find something positive to come out of all the long years of contact with the family is an important comment on the difficulties of working effectively where practitioners deal with high numbers of complex and chronically bad cases. One might however ask the question as to what this relationship achieved, and what was the price for its sustenance? You have here a situation that is chronically bad, where there is little evidence of any positive change in the parent's drug use or home situation. The social worker had gained access to the family home, where initially she had not, and the relationship had developed such that now the parents would admit to taking drugs. However, as she herself notes, this is really about the limit of it. The same social worker also described a recent home visit to this family where she nearly sat on a used syringe and needle left lying sticking upright. If the house was like this when the family knew she was visiting, and could be presumed to have a heightened presentational awareness, what would it be like on every other day in terms of child safety and care? As this health visitor commented:

But you're only ever getting a snapshot at, you know, that half an hour or whatever that you're actually in the house as to whether all that is in place all the rest of the time?

(Health visitor 1: FG7)

Was the trade off for gaining access a situation that increasingly precluded the social worker from challenging the family circumstance, so that, in effect, it was the family who set the agenda? The point is underlined by the recent Caleb Ness fatal inquiry in Scotland, where the *apparent* co-operation of the mother had clouded the lead social worker's judgement as to the safety of the child. In not being critical, the mother had great scope to manage the impression that her son was safe (O'Brien *et al.* 2003). And again, the recent 'Inspection into the Care and Protection of Children of Eilean Sar' in Scotland cautions that the willingness of parents to co-operate with workers is not in itself an indication of improved parenting (Social Work Inspection Agency 2005). Chronically bad situations, like those often prompted by drug problems, can engender low expectations of change in clients. These, in turn, can create an over-reliance on proxy markers of change that can mask a dangerously deteriorating situation for children.

Decision-making processes: A vignette

The following vignette, which was discussed by practitioners in all the focus groups, is illustrative of the situational nature of decision-making and the processes by which child welfare can become sidelined. The vignette describes a mother who has gone to the methadone clinic with her ten-year-old son and her six-month-old daughter. She has been on a methadone prescription for a year and, over the last few visits, has been obviously under the influence of more than her methadone. This time, however, she is barely compos mentis; her son is watching over the baby and also looking after his mother. All of the focus group participants, irrespective of profession, saw that this potentially represented a child protection issue; their attention was particularly drawn to the baby's potential vulnerability; as has been noted elsewhere, older children are more likely to escape notice (Taylor and Kroll 2004). The practitioners were largely agreed that the situation described by the vignette would probably necessitate, at some point, the involvement of social work. However their responses differed as to what to do about the immediate situation. Those drug workers with a principally adult-focused remit were the most likely to try to resolve the problem in-house in the first instance, favouring a wait and see approach, despite the fact that the mother was clearly currently incapable whilst responsible for the two children. There was a reticence to do something that would ratchet up the problem by involving social work at this stage and a corresponding search for mitigating reasons *not* to act but retain a watching brief. The worst of this was to look to the ten-year-old boy to keep things ticking over:

> I would look at putting her medication up. Again I would ask if there was anyone else in the family [to take care of the children] but the way I'm looking at it, this ten-year-old seems to be doing a not too bad a job at lifting the baby and stuff like that and it might be okay for a couple of days until this new methadone kicks in. I don't think I would feel the need to take the baby into care straight away.
>
> (Drug worker 1: FG2)

The inclination to rely on the caring capacities of a ten year old was unusual. However, the drive to contain the situation was not. The first response was most likely to be one of finding a means of ameliorating the present situation (contact the extended family, review the methadone dose, put in some home support), and, then to review the situation:

> I think most of the time this would be discussed either with a colleague in the addiction staff and it would be left to see what was the outcome of the next week is going to be or, if it was important they would get in

touch with a senior social worker. That's taken a long, long time for us to be able to do that. Again, geographically we are in the same building, we have better relationships with the social work department than I think most. But we're also very, we don't jump in there.

(Drug worker 1: FG1)

The search for mitigating reasons that would allow the practitioner to view the adult's incapacity as a temporary problem to be resolved, and therefore not necessarily a decision about child safety, was also a feature of the drug workers' response to the situation:

I mean I think as an addiction worker I wouldn't be looking for them [other addiction workers] to look too much at parenting. I think just looking at the woman and why is she topping up on methadone? What's going on for her in her life that she is needing to top up and therefore not able to be on the ball to look after the wee one? It might be that the ex is on the scene or the husband is on the scene and that is stressful, and it is about talking to her about that. It is about addressing what is going on for her that makes her need to top up and by doing that I think you are addressing maybe that parenting by the fact that she's maybe feels the need now to top up that it is no, she can cope a lot better on a script. And it might be that she is fine with her parenting it's just that she is topping up because of other stresses, it's about looking at her first as the adult, or the person, and about looking at that.

(Drug worker 2: FG2)

This was also true of some of the social workers. The appearance of the children was taken as an important marker, particularly focused on the state of their clothes, as was the straightforward interpretation of the vignette, made by a number of individuals across the practitioner groups, that having been on a methadone prescription for the past year equated with stability. An example of this is cited below, as is the more questioning response of another social worker in the focus group:

SW1: I think she's done well if she's been on methadone for a year to keep things going then. With a boy age ten and a baby girl of six months, she should be commended for that, I think.

SW2: But I think there is, I would say, is she keeping things going or is she just keeping up a pretence because the boy seems to be assuming a not-an-age-appropriate role in relation to supporting his mother and the child?

(Social workers 1 and 2: FG8)

Clearly these are all possibilities and would need to be taken into account in any subsequent review. One can see that although these workers were clear that there was a problem and most wanted social work to be informed, they were also actively engaged in a search for a more optimistic interpretation of the situation to allow a more informal response:

> I: So, like you said earlier, you wouldn't go in blue lights flashing over something like this?
>
> DW2: No, not at that stage. I think obviously the woman needs some time to follow it up the next day when she is a bit straighter, try and find out how much she has been using, is there a particular reason why? Is there a real stress around for her at the moment, 'em and try and you know support her.
>
> (Drug worker 2: FG4)

What one sees in these responses is a subtle, yet significant, shift away from addressing the immediate child protection issues, to focus on the mother's rationale for increased drug use. The attendant assumption is that given time (next day, next week) the practitioner can address the mother's stress and, in so doing, sort things out for the children. The focus on the mother, however, distracts attention away from the saliency of the child protection concerns.

Another important factor influencing the response of practitioners to the situation was the relative case. The following practitioner's assessment of the vignette situation was in terms of the rest of his caseload:

> This kind of a thing, as I say, is like normal for us, so it wouldn't ring any bells. It would need to be something a lot worse than that before we would access someone.
>
> (Drug worker 1: FG2)

The adoption of a 'wait and see' approach to avoid formalizing the problem means the immediate problem of the mother's incapacity has to be dealt with informally and within the resources of the staff present. In a busy clinic such resources might be thinly stretched which, as the following drug worker acknowledged, could mean it was not addressed:

> I: Would you think that there is any chance that the child looking after this child, this baby, would ever pass unnoticed in any of your services?
>
> DW2: It could do yes if we were extremely busy and I think 'oh yes I must have a look at that, must catch up on that, must do something about it', and then you've got another crisis or something else happening.

DW1: Because there are times when things are noticeable and nothing seems to be done and it depends on the pressure of work.

DW2: At the methadone clinic you don't have much time with each person and you, I think you would probably be very much at the front of your mind that you had a great big queue of people sitting outside waiting to see you as well.

(Drug workers 1 and 2: FG2)

Although practical constraints of time and service capacity clearly have a role to play over practitioners' capabilities to respond, this was not the whole of it. Dingwall and colleagues have previously noted a preference in the structures of organizations involved in child welfare and in the practical reasoning of its members for 'the least stigmatising interpretation of the available data and the least overtly coercive possible disposition' (1983). Something of the same preference was evident in these focus groups, which was, at least partially, motivated by a concern with the maintenance of the adult relationship as the prime vehicle for retaining clients' engagement with agencies. The effect however, could be that the child's needs for protection were elided.

Relationships between practitioners

Effective communication and joint working between agencies to protect children is notoriously difficult (Kroll and Taylor 2003; Lalayants and Epstein 2005). Unsurprisingly then, these focus groups were replete with examples of the fracture lines between practitioners, the most acute of which was in the setting apart of social work. Health visiting and drug services were framed as voluntary and preventive, but social work was framed in terms of its coercive powers to intervene. On the one hand, this meant that all roads led to social work once it was perceived that the situation had gone beyond prevention. On the other, the authority invested in the office of social work was, to an extent, resented.

Two major sources of resentment were identifiable; the first concerned the perception that social workers expected other practitioners to act as their eyes and ears and police their clients. The second concerned the potential treatment of a case once it had passed onto social work. Both issues connected intimately with their continued engagement with the adult client and/or children. The following health visitor provided a clear example of this:

We're supposed to work as part of a multi-disciplinary group and I think sometimes the social work department have unrealistic expectations as to what, or they don't know what the role of the health visitor is and just because they're not getting access they think that we can demand rights of access in to a home. And I, I feel as, I don't always necessarily get access into a home but if they come to me at the clinic, which some of them do, I content myself with that, that I'm getting contact with the family and I don't want to break down the relationship that I have by demanding access into their home, I don't have any right to access, I'm invited into their homes.

(Health visitor 3: FG9)

The social workers in the focus groups confirmed this expectation that practitioners should monitor and report concerns to them, because of their statutory responsibilities to protect children. They acknowledged their limited access to families and reliance upon other practitioners, particularly health visitors, to keep a watching brief. With regard to services offered by drug workers they could see the merits of a division of labour in working with parents and children:

They (drug workers) probably get the best or the most out of the client that they're working with, because we certainly don't, we get a lot of the superficial stuff and a lot of the stuff that goes with the myths – you know that the first time that they slip up we are just going to snatch those children away from them.

(Social worker 1: FG6)

However this was not entirely straightforward as, to some social workers at least, there was the perception that they became locked into a good guy–bad guy routine. This was particularly felt where the referring practitioner did not want the client to know that they had rung the alarm bells:

SW3: …they (other practitioners) like the good relationship with the parent, and the bad social worker comes up and does all the bad things.

SW4: It's a bit like, they'll give us ammunition but you're the ones that have to fire it.

(SW3 and 4: FG5)

Again this was couched in terms of the referring practitioner's concern to retain the relationship. Health visitors too found themselves in this situation; they reported being asked, in particular by teachers, to refer welfare problems to the social work department. This dynamic was objected to on the grounds that in shrugging off responsibility it was playing them off against the client and to an extent was perceived as collusive, divisive and not in the best interests of the child. That some drug workers and health visitors also made mention of a lack of information from social work to them can perhaps be taken as indicative of the general point that communication between practitioners has the potential to be fraught.

Damned if you do and damned if you don't

A recurrently raised problem for the referring workers (whether drug workers or health visitors) was that in transferring the case to social work, there was the possibility of a different interpretation of how best to respond to the case. Most commonly for drug workers was uneasiness over a narrow focus on a child protection agenda. There was the expressed anxiety that the response might be overly coercive:

> I would obviously be quite reluctant [to refer this vignette case] in case, you know, the social work department decided that she wasn't capable of looking after her kids, and the implication's there, because unfortunately the social workers tell clients, I've seen this, that cruelty…they're going to take your weans away, kind of thing, you know. And I think that part of our job is to get them to understand that that's not the case, that's always a last resort. That's a big part of our job.
>
> (Drug worker 3: FG4)

There was also the worry, often based on past experience, that there might not be any response at all. Families who end up being referred to social work rarely greet it with anything other than fear and anger, at least initially. They may have a sense of having been betrayed by the worker making the referral. It is a price that workers will pay once they are sure there is a problem that requires further notification. If, however, their referral to social work does not result in the case being allocated and there is no provision of a service, then the drug worker or health visitor has jeopardized, without result, their access to the family and with it the opportunity to keep a watching brief on the children. This was experienced both as frustrating and dangerous and quite possibly affected their judgement as to how bad a case had to be to refer onwards.

> I don't know about you but sometimes you feel as if…I mean you can't phone social workers and say, you know, this person's using a bit more heavily. They're looking for something more concrete than that, so sometimes I…I've been in a few situations where I felt I've just been almost like an observer and watched. You know I've been going in and

saying 'this isn't good if you're using' or 'we really...' you know just going on, you sort of just watch the whole thing until things get to such a state where social work have really no choice but to get involved. I can think of at least two occasions in the last two years where I felt I was in that situation.

(Health visitor 2: FG7)

And:

Just about a year ago I was on the phone all the time, wrote letters to social work, but they never respond to you and then it did all explode you know and I felt isolated being the only worker going into this home and no one would really take my referral seriously enough until there was a crisis and then the police, they had to get an order for care and protection and then children in hospital by that point, too late...two drug dependent parents. I was very, very concerned.

(Health visitor 3: FG9)

Children and family social work services in the UK are chronically under-staffed; the remaining staff are often demotivated and stressed by the volume of work, and the strain of working with difficult, frequently highly conflictual and chronic child protection cases. Many of the drug workers and health visitors expressed their sense of social work as a service in crisis, with extremely limited capacity to respond to anything other than the worst child protection cases, triggered usually by incidents rather than the chronic accumulation of problems:

DW1: Unfortunately because resources have deteriorated and workers have far higher caseloads it's a lot of just crisis intervention. You know things get left and left and left until you're at the point where you know the kids are ready to come into care because nothing's been done prior to that.

DW2: That's right, that's what we find, we were talking about the blue lights flashing, once that starts, that's when you'll get your, you know what I mean [social work support], it's got to get to that point most of the time.

(Drug workers 1 and 2: FG1)

Such a situation creates a dangerous grey area with regard to the safety and care of children and is a particularly likely scenario in cases of neglect. As has been argued throughout this chapter, the emphasis placed on the practitioner/client relationship, and the drive to view the situation in its most optimistic light, might very well mean a situation that has already greatly deteriorated before referral occurs. Yet if the social work department is only really able to respond to those cases readily identified as presenting a serious risk to children (usually incidents of actual harm), it suggests a worrying number of children who 'fall through the gaps', whose circumstances are chronically detrimental. Moreover, as already indicated, uncertainty amongst other practitioners as to whether or not a case is bad enough to receive due attention might further elevate their own thresholds of reportable risk.

Conclusion

The purpose of this chapter has been to draw awareness to the ways in which practitioners' relationships with their adult clients, and with each other, have the capacity to distract attention away from the child. At best a good relationship with a client may be a critical ingredient in bringing about positive change, at its worst it may be no more than a powerful bit of impression management, allowing the client scope to direct the relationship with the practitioner (Reder *et al.* 2003). For good or ill, practitioners rely on these relationships to do their work; indeed they are integral to it. Running alongside this is the organizational directive to think the best of clients that is enshrined in the UK Children Acts (England and Wales 1989; Scotland 1995), which place great emphasis on minimal intervention and family preservation. In combination these are forceful currents that can ironically lead to a situation that is, perhaps, 'overly respectful of parental liberties' (Dingwall *et al.* 1983) at the expense of the care and wellbeing of children. This is one of the most recurrent themes in inquiries into child fatalities and the problem that most greatly needs attention.

It is perhaps ironic that in all the crowded attention on the parent with the drug problem throughout these focus groups, there was very little discussion among the practitioners of the children's perspectives. For the most part their needs were assumed, and considered to be best met through supporting the parent. This might be an explicable dynamic, especially where children are very young, but it creates a dangerous invisibility and reinforces their vulnerability.

The next and final chapter looks at current policy and provision for families affected by drugs and asks the rhetorical question as to whether we can just keep on tinkering with the current system or whether it requires fundamental overhaul.

Chapter 10

Conclusion: What Needs to Happen: A Case of Tinkering or Overhaul?

Written with Joy Barlow

Introduction

The story of drugs in the family was not a happy one for anyone who told it here. In their experience, drug dependence brought immense conflict and strain, was profoundly disruptive and a cause of deep lasting misery and shame. It drove a wedge between mothers and fathers, brothers and sisters, grandparents and parents. It contributed to ill health and mental stress and left vulnerable, damaged and unhappy children in its wake. It is therefore all the more astonishing to realize that a theme common to every chapter in this book has been a turning away from the disaster, whether from institutional blindness, or indifference, or through prioritizing the needs of the problem drug user over those affected by the drug problem.

For far too long the needs of these families have gone unrecognized and unmet. Even discounting the sheer weight of human misery brought about by a family member's drug problem, one might think its translation into economic cost through the physical and mental ill health of parents and grandparents, through distressed and disturbed children, through inter- and cross-generational transmission of drug problems, would be a strong impetus for concerted action. That it has not is testimony to an enduring fiction that drugs and drug treatment are about the mind and body of the person taking them. This has to change, but how and by how much? Is it really feasible to expect that policies and practices philosophically founded on the individual could expand to incorporate a broader, much messier vision of family function and family relationships as dynamic, not static, as active and reactive?

What would it take for things really to change? The first essential shift has to be engaging with the damage that a family member's drug problem creates for families and their children. This looks at first glance to be deceptively simple but, of course, as with most human things, it is not. The delivery of drug treatment and other services, in the UK at least, is philosophically underpinned by policies premised upon being non-judgemental and inclusive. Considered just in terms of the presenting individual this seems relatively unproblematic. However, it becomes less straightforward when one starts to take into account the ways in which the individual with the drug problem affects those close to them. Much as people have the right to not be stigmatized or marginalized for their drug problems, this right does not release them from responsibility for the damage that their drug use causes to others. It should be integral to the working practice of agencies working with problem drug users that these rights to be treated humanely and with respect come with responsibility for the maintenance of these same rights for others. The common characterization of people with drug problems as society's victims derives in part from the will to avoid moral judgement of their behaviour as intrinsically bad. Cloaking problem drug use in amorality, however, has made it increasingly difficult to 'see' the victims of the victim: in this case their families and children.

For the sake of clarity, this chapter will divide between first considering the merits and importance of acknowledging philosophically and practically that drugs are not just the problem of the presenting individual, but of their families too. It will then focus on the particular problems encountered by children of parents who are drug dependent. Inevitably the greater potential vulnerability of children of parents with drug problems imposes a necessary hierarchy of need and response. The important point however, is that the protection and welfare of such children is not just about the parent and the child but about the extended family too.

Working with the family

Even the slightest contact with the numerous support groups for families of substance misusers all over the UK leaves one with the clear sense that these groups for the most part exist despite, not because of, drug policy and strategy. They are often self-supporting and run on a shoestring.

For the most part they appear to be set up by parents affected by their children's drug problems and framed in terms of the support that parents can offer to each other in trying to navigate the turbulence of living with their child's drug problem. Even where such groups are located in close proximity to drug services, there is often little dialogue between the two.

Why is this? At least part of the reason seems to reside in the well-rehearsed belief that the family caused the problem in the first place through dysfunction and abuse. Many people with drug problems report terrible childhoods marked by parental alcohol or drug use, by neglect or physical or sexual abuse. If this is the case, what could be the possible rationale for any further involvement of the extended family?

The first point one might make, however, is that such dismissal tars all families with the same brush, which is simply not warranted. The routes young people take into problem drug misuse are not confined to the existence of severe family problems, particularly given that so many children grow up in communities where the full range of illegal drugs is highly prevalent.

Second, family structures change over time and so too do family processes, sometimes for the better. The past, although significant, does not have to determine the future.

Third, for better or worse the problem drug user is part of their family and it is this family that is very likely to play a crucial role in shaping the destiny of that drug user. Indeed the family is frequently a good deal more significant and influential than any drug or social welfare agency will ever be. Recognition of the part played by family dysfunction in influencing the drug career trajectory offers an important opportunity to work with, rather than against, relational dynamics and family problems.

A policy move away from framing the harms of problem drug use in individual terms towards their greater contextualization within families would obviously carry with it many resource and organizational implications. Not the least of these would be to train practitioners to work within a more expansive vision of drug-related harm. This might be helped where family support groups could be co-located with drug agencies and serious efforts made to create synergy based on a perhaps differently framed, but still common, purpose. There are clearly many difficulties with engaging families and clearly too not all families would want, or know how, to become involved in such a process. Some families too would be impossible to work with. However without throwing the baby out with the bathwater, there will still be a sizeable number of families that want to find the means to help their child and who would benefit from some help themselves in the struggle to do so.

The stigma associated with having a problem drug user in the family and the sense that a family problem should be resolvable within the family, usually translates into isolation and stress as families try to cope, often over many years. Early contact with families could help them to capitalize on their strengths and assist them in understanding how drug careers often progress and the implications of this for their family. It would be particularly important in this respect to draw on the experiences of other parents to guard against the tendency to become so fully occupied with the drug problem of one child, that the needs of their other children are eclipsed. The relative lack of attention paid to other siblings can set in train behaviours that create skewed family dynamics, but also increase the vulnerability of these siblings to drug exposure and initiation. Practitioners working with problem drug use have an educative role to play too since it is clear that many problem drug users are, perhaps unintentionally, modelling drug use for their younger siblings. There is potential here for a good deal of collaborative work that can be carried out with, not despite, families. This might over time alleviate some of the problems for drug users and their families and, at the least, provide them with some indication of the long journey ahead.

The potential merit of harnessing the power of the family to change things for the better is perhaps best evidenced in the broad church of multi-systemic family therapies directed at young people whose behaviours have become problematic: that familiar cocktail of alcohol and illegal drug use, disengagement from school and increasing involvement with juvenile justice. These (mostly US-based) therapies are premised on the notion that a young person's behaviour is greatly influenced by complex interactions between family, friends and environment. Young people can become locked into increasingly negative patterns of behaviour, often located in conflictual family relationships and reinforced by negative patterns of action and reaction. Through identifying and working with such dynamics these therapies aim to break the cycles of negative behaviour and divert young people away from drug problems and criminality. Moreover, rigourous evaluation of these interventions indicates they are effective in preventing an escalation of problem behaviours (Liddle et al. 2001; Williams and Chang 2000).

This more integrative approach, however, is still primarily focused on the individual as the unit of change; the family member with the developing drug problem is still at the centre of the web. Consideration of the more indirect effects of living with a family member's drug problem is still missing in this schema, yet is a significant cause of family strain in its own right. These strains appear to contribute to health-related problems in parents, and in affecting family cohesion and parental attention may also contribute to the increased risk of siblings being drug exposed. The economic and social costs of not responding to the negative impacts of drug problems on other family members seem likely to be high and are another key argument for trying to find means of amelioration. One might suggest the potential value of initiating means of providing respite to families through offering time away, or developing mentoring services for siblings. These are not costly options yet they are helpful, and more so for their recognition of the heavy toll exacted by a close family member's drug problem. It is not easy to be prescriptive about what ought to happen to provide better help for families. Clearly many families are doing it for themselves through their membership of family support groups. The existence of these groups does offer some means of channelling support or greater integration within the framework of drug services. A more solid commitment would signal to family support networks their legitimacy, which is often lacking given that they generally exist on a shoestring budget and are frequently sustained largely though the voluntary efforts of their membership. Equally, the onus is on drug services to find means of including families in their work where possible, rather than following the current practice of treating the drug user in isolation from their family.

Nonetheless, suggesting that the family becomes the unit of interest is altogether a much less tractable proposition. All that conflict, all those problems built up over many years need skill and commitment to try to unravel. The complexities in family make-up, their often turbulent histories and reticence to come forward publicly with their problems, all add to the difficulties of judging what might be the best way to proceed. Yet since these problems exist irrespective of whether or not there is an effort to address them, the question really revolves around whether there is the will and the expertise to do so.

The section that follows looks at the particular implications for policy and practice where children of parents with drug problems are concerned.

Working with children and families

In this book, parents, children and the extended family all described the often-realized potential for parental drug problems to have a negative impact on child wellbeing and safety. In its most extreme form it leads to children whose lives are lost, but all along the way it creates emotional damage that cripples these young lives, sometimes forever. The international literature largely confirms this probability, particularly where parental drug use is uncontrolled. It is this *potential* for problems with parenting that is so important to focus upon, and the effects on children who grow up in the midst of the incipient unpredictability that characterizes problem drug-using careers. Even in the course of a single day, it is possible to see many instances where the imperative to attend to the needs of the drug habit conflicts with attending to children's needs for routine and predictability.

Looking the problem in the eye

The 'potentiality' of parental drug problems to damage children leads one to fundamentally question the often quoted – but not much evidenced – statement that 'being a problem drug using parent does not necessarily mean an inability to parent' (Mountenay 1998). The problem with this statement is that whilst comfortingly non-judgemental, it is frequently interpreted to mean that there is no particular effect attributable to problem drug use. Yet the evidence just does not stack up in support of this assertion. One might agree with the use of the caveat 'necessarily' but add that it is only under conditions of stringently controlled drug use (whatever the substance) that parental capacity will not be impeded to the detriment of the child. To assert that parental drug problems are bad for children's welfare begins a bold and somewhat uncompromising conversation that turns the tables on the present tendency for policy and practice to be reactive. On the contrary what are needed are systems that are fine tuned to anticipating problems. The Laming Report on the death of Victoria Climbié (Lord Laming 2003), for example, noted that professionals were too prepared to accept information at face value and recommended that frontline workers should instead adopt a routine position of 'respectful uncertainty' with clients. Even this sounds rather hesitant in the face of the need for frontline workers to adopt an almost forensic approach to what they see and hear in their contact with families if they are to maintain a focus on the safety of the child independent of parental agendas. A sceptical outlook and a readiness to challenge information given by parents and other professionals might have been critical in saving the lives of both Victoria Climbié in England and Caleb Ness in Scotland. Crucially, too, there has to be more stringent dialogue about outcomes for these children and the limits to supporting families.

Currently the kinds of interventions one most often sees are about supporting families through trying to change things for the parent, the assumption being that a happier parent will result in a happier, safer child. One can see this, for example, in the plethora of interventions to alleviate stress for parents. Partly this has arisen out of the legal framework governing child protection, which stresses the importance of family preservation. Agencies have operated on the model that a child's best interests are met through staying in the family home and accordingly the emphasis has been on relieving many of the sources of stress for the parent (which, at its worst, has meant the state effectively parenting the child through provision of round the clock support). Partly too, the effort to avoid stigmatizing problem drug use has created great moral uncertainty over the legitimacy of intervening at all in the sphere of the family, particularly amongst those concerned with adult clients. The rhetoric of supporting families (which frequently is taken to mean supporting the parent) offers a less obviously conflictual, more acceptable route than is implied by a stance premised on the likelihood that drugs are causing problems for children's welfare.

The speed with which things can turn for the worse in drug-affected households underlines the imperative for high levels of watchfulness and reactivity. Setting in place systems geared to early identification of parenting in the context of problem drug use, and the active monitoring and tracking of such families, offers agencies the prospect of earlier intervention where children become caught in escalating drug use and its attendant chaos. Whilst such systems might be premised on being supportive and facilitative, there needs also to be clarity over how and when to act where situations worsen.

Swift action and the institution of time frames

At every stage the onus on parents should be to demonstrate that they are able to provide a safe and caring rearing environment for their children. Having in place precise protocols on which the relevant staff are fully trained to understand their role in relation to the protection of children would greatly help staff to recognize the signs of a deteriorating circumstance for children and, importantly, provide clear guidance on how to act. Of equal importance to training staff, however, is ensuring the adequacy of an emotionally supportive infrastructure for them in the face of increased potential for conflicts with clients where there is greater assertion of standards of parenting.

Recognition of the damage that parental drug misuse can create for children's wellbeing requires an explicit commitment not just to supporting families but also to acting decisively once it is clear that a parent is persistently failing to attend to their child's needs for wellbeing and safety. It is not a question of prejudice governing action, it is not about how nice or otherwise that parent might be, it is about ensuring that children being raised in these families are better supported and less vulnerable than the evidence currently indicates, and that the limits to family preservation are institutionally clearly acknowledged and acted upon. Many of these children simply ought not to be left in the care of their parents if they persist in following the routes of their drug problems. When drugs come first, there is no safe place for children, particularly if they are young and vulnerable.

The institution of clear time frames that are understood by parents, enforced by agencies and have legal sanction would help to keep attention focused on the need for momentum. In every case the preferred option should be for parents to work towards abstinence from drugs, as this offers children their best hope of stability. The US 'Adoption and Safe Families Act' (ASFA) (O'Flynn 1999) offers some direction in this regard, as this legislation was precisely targeted to address the problems created where parents fail over time to meet their parental responsibilities and children are left in limbo in the care system. ASFA set a time frame for parents to make and sustain positive change from the point at which a child is received into care. If a child is in care for 15 out of 22 of the proceeding months then permanency proceedings should be initiated. The introduction of a defined endpoint may seem draconian, however, it is important that one keeps the child in mind. A life lived with drugs with all its attendant chaos causes enormous damage to children, as does a situation where children come into and out of care throughout all their young lives. Furthermore the evidence from the US suggests that the time-limited opportunity to retain parental rights over children has been a spur to many to make life changes (O'Flynn 1999; Semidei *et al*. 2001). This is a positive outcome and preferable to having to remove the child from parental care and seek their adoption with another family. However, preference for this outcome should not be confused with the main purpose of the ASFA, which was to stop the damaging seesaw of children coming in and out of the care system because their parents were chronically unable to provide a stable nurturing environment.

The onus is therefore on parents to become drug free if they want to retain their parental rights. The flip side of this is the attendant responsibility of the state to ensure adequate provision of drug rehabilitation facilities to assist this journey. A policy premised on stringent outcomes will have no legitimacy where it is not matched by an equivalent commitment to provide people with the help they need to become drug free. Where parents access this help and still cannot meet their responsibilities to their children, it is right that alternative arrangements should be made for those children.

Anxieties over the care system

Professional chariness over reporting child maltreatment for fear of negative consequences, whether for the child or for parental treatment attendance, has been well documented (Alvarez *et al*. 2005). More deeply, there is the sense of family that most of us carry within us, whether real or imagined. We hold dear to family, see it as our irreducible core for good or ill, and for this reason are deeply suspicious of alternatives. For all the reiteration of the harm and misery that drugs had caused by parents, grandparents and, most especially, by children and young people, it is still the most difficult thing to say that children should be taken away from their mothers or fathers and brought into care. It is much easier to talk about placing children with grandparents and other relatives because they are family and so it is less of a wrench for everyone, professionals included. However, the recommendation that more of these children ought to be taken from their drug-using parents and, if necessary, received into foster care or various other kinds of care homes or, more finally, placed for adoption, has a certain inescapable brutality about it. It is a difficult thing to say, and all *we* are doing *is* saying it. How much more difficult for those working at the sharp end with these families and having to face parents and children who cling to each other, and to the notion that more time, more support will change things?

The reluctance of many practitioners, particularly those working primarily with adults, to address the issue of child welfare unless absolutely necessary is likely to be linked to a fear of the consequences. The spectre of having to involve social work and initiating a train of events possibly leading to taking the child into care can be a deterrent to action. Social workers may dread introducing yet more conflict into their work and may indeed be afraid of physical threats from angry parents (Ferguson 2005). The problem is that this reticence, however born, can lead to dangerous drift, leaving children in chronically bad circumstances that grind on and on until finally, when the damage has been done, they are removed anyway. In this way children are failed, first by their parents and then by the systems that are supposedly designed to protect them. There is a growing body of evidence that challenges the reticence to act on the basis of a necessarily gloomy prognosis. Practitioners often worry that they will lose their adult clients if they talk about their children. However, research on the treatment retention of clients who have been reported for child maltreatment found, on the contrary, that for the great majority there was either no change to the professional–client relationship, or it was in fact improved (Watson and Levine 1989; Weinstein *et al.* 2000). Furthermore, many clients were reportedly relieved that their childcare problems were brought into the open and explicitly addressed (Alvarez *et al.* 2005). Intervention was also judged by many of these clients to have led to a better life for the family.

There is an important need for training with professionals that confronts the evidence base of some of these assertions because of their effects on practice. Allied to this is the importance of addressing head on the complex emotions that go hand in hand with this work and which can be a significant barrier to practitioners raising child welfare concerns with clients (Ferguson 2005). In particular, attention needs to be paid to professional cultures within which child protection work happens. Conflict needs to be recognized as an inherent constituent of social care work given that a significant number of clients will neither invite nor accept intervention willingly. How this plays out in professional life will be greatly affected by the supportive infrastructures within which workers operate. The readiness of workers to confront conflictual situations, and their ability to operate effectively within them, must be less where they work in chronically under-staffed, under-resourced offices with little scope for concomitant professional development and guidance.

The disquiet that many professionals report at the care options available to children if they are taken away from parental care inevitably plays a part in their decision-making. Year on year there are fewer people willing to take on fostering of children, care homes are known to be problematic and residential schools are, among other things, very expensive. Furthermore, a number of court cases in recent years have brought to light the potential for misuse of power by carers who have abused these already damaged children. Nonetheless, is weighing up bad against worse the best we can do? How can the answer be to leave them in circumstances that are judged to be less damaging, often on the basis that family, for all its faults, might be better than some form of out of home care? Children deserve far better than a choice between lesser evils: the onus must be on greatly improving the type and quality of out of home care that they receive. There simply have to be good models of care out there, in the UK and further afield. It must be possible to provide a better and more nurturing environment for a child than an emotionally barren and often dangerous place that is home in name only.

Going back through the study interviews carried out with children and young people it is not surprising to find that most of those children who lived with their parents were fearful of being separated and taken into care. However, two points are important here; first, very many of these children stated that they would have welcomed intervention that took their needs into account. Most felt they had, in fact, been ignored, even when there had been agency intervention. Second, of those children and young people who had been taken into care, their experience was not necessarily bad. There was often a sense of relief to be out of an increasingly distressing situation and to be in a different and safer place, even while missing their parent(s).

It is noteworthy that one rigorously controlled study of developmental and behavioural outcomes for adopted children of problem drug-using parents found these to be much better than among children who had remained with their parents (Ornoy et al. 1996). There is a lamentable lack of properly designed research on what happens over time to children who are permanently removed from their family homes, compared to those left in them. However the point to be made here is that the assertion that children are better off in their families ought to be tested each time. An essential part of this testing has to be the placement of the child's needs at the centre of any investigation. It requires courage to affirm that family preservation should not be the default position, and this has to be matched by a properly financed commitment to changing the care system into something better than the worst option.

Recommending that we should be less reticent about the use of adoption and fostering where parents are unable to meet their responsibilities for the care and safety of their children may seem brutal. However, it is our view based on everything in this book and in our considerable research and practical experience, that parental drug use is severely detrimental to children where it is not stringently controlled. To us, the greater brutality is that so many children's lives have been so blighted and that, in our reluctance to see, we have turned again and again from the chance to change that.

Supporting extended family carers

It is in recognition of the dangers posed to child welfare by parental drug problems that so many children are placed with the extended family, whether by the parents themselves or by the state. The obvious advantage is that children are still in their families, if not with their parents. However, as we have seen, whilst grandparents and other relatives take on this responsibility and many would fight for the right to do so, it comes at a price that, even with the best will in the world, is often heavy. There are financial and other costs of raising children who are often greatly damaged by what they have experienced and present all sorts of behavioural problems that are difficult to manage.

Despite legal wrangling on the precise differences between kinship and foster care, the bottom line is that these grandparents, aunts and uncles, etc. are caring for children who need to be sheltered, fed and clothed. It is a travesty that the financial costs of these are borne largely alone by relatives but met by the state for foster carers. Also, the strains associated with fostering are institutionally recognized and supported, whilst family members who take on this care are often left to their own devices, or to seek out each other for support, in the absence of any other formal recognition of what they have taken on. The lack of financial and other assistance can undermine the ability and faith of family members to retain their role as the primary carer, putting these already vulnerable children at risk of yet more instability. Since the extended family is so often all that stands between children and the care system, there ought to be formal recognition and support of this assumption of parental responsibility.

If the price for state payment is that there is much greater oversight of the care provided by relatives, then so be it. Indeed a good case can be made for introducing more robust means of assessing the supportive capacities of kin carers. It certainly was no disincentive to the grandparents in this study, many of whom were precariously close to the edge financially for much of the time. The needs of these children for a nurturing, stable and caring environment are all the more acute where they have come from environments lacking these essentials. A blood tie is not of itself any guarantee that a child will be nurtured; certainly the high levels of neglect and abuse retrospectively reported by problem drug users at the hands of their own parents have to give pause to any such uncritical assertion. Whilst accepting that events deep in the past may have no necessary bearing on circumstances today, the argument for a close look at the present day capabilities of kinship carers still holds good. At the same time, grandparents and other relatives will not willingly accept such scrutiny unless it is allied to the provision of concrete support.

Safe havens

With the best will in the world, these institutional measures to better protect children will not be able to plug all the gaps left where parents have been unable to provide stable and nurturing home lives. The sheer press of their numbers is indicative of the likely problems of accommodating to their needs. As much as it is important to institute measures to identify family problems early and act decisively to try to resolve them, so too should there be some independent attention paid to meeting children's needs away from their families and more on their own terms.

For all the rhetoric of putting children first, it is astonishing that so few services apparently exist that are centred on the child directly. The default position is one of 'treat the parent and you treat the child'. This has an obvious logic where one is considering very young, dependent children, however, it holds less and less as children get older. In this respect one might think of a situation where a parent is coming off drugs, or stabilizing on methadone and assuming a more active parental role. On the face of it one would assume that this is a good thing, however, particularly for an older child it might mean unwelcome attention and supervision where previously they had been largely self-determining. This changed dynamic might precipitate a negative reaction on the part of the young person, as was found to be the case in research by Catalano and colleagues (1999) in evaluating an intervention that had led to quite significant reductions in problem drug use by parents, as well as the instigation of more family meetings and rules. From the point of view of older children, these changes in family functioning were unwelcome and their own behaviours were apt to worsen. It is not enough to attempt to fix things for the parent; children's needs are not necessarily perfectly aligned with those of their parents.

Perhaps so few services are aimed at children from troubled backgrounds because they are challenging; they have many needs, they are often angry and confused and these spill inevitably into all areas of their lives. These angers, fears and anxieties, their defensiveness and possibly mental health problems may easily be roused and less easily quelled. Providing an arena within which children find acceptance even despite the display of behaviours that are disruptive and sometimes destructive, is fundamentally about care, commitment and skill. These havens might take different forms, but share the aim of providing nurturance and care in a supportive environment, starting with the basics like food and help with clothing, through to sorting out problems with schools and criminal justice. Above all, such places need to be able to offer children a chance to be in a safe, caring environment where their own homes are not.

Some of the best examples of these safe havens appear to exist within the voluntary sector; perhaps this is significant. Working with these children requires a commitment to flexibility across time and in approach that defies the more tightly defined working hours, job descriptions, performance indicators and targets characteristic of many statutory sector funded projects. Linked to this are the ways in which children gain access to these projects. Where children need to be referred to services there is first the problem that not all children who could benefit from these kinds of services are known about. Second, the attendant labelling may be sufficient to put them off accessing it anyway. A child-referred service may be more difficult bureaucratically but it does place the onus firmly on that service to make sure that they are offering something that children really want and might benefit from enough to actually attend.

A further crucial element in working with children from damaged backgrounds is that some are going to act out; they may at times be ungracious about your kind efforts to help them, they may damage property when they are angry and be rude and abusive. In the worst of times, these things may all come as a package. These behaviours cause children to be excluded from school and other mainstream services, and, are part of their journey of narrowing options. If, however, it is understood that these behaviours are a symptom not a cause of their problems, then the last thing such a service can do is give up on them too. This is not the same as what in social work speak is termed 'unconditional positive regard'. Regard should be positive but it should not be unconditional. As in life generally, action comes with consequences and these need to be faced up to. But whatever the sanction, the important point is that the service remains open to the child and that this is the case for the long haul. This is a tough call, given just how difficult some behaviour can be to contain. Nonetheless, it is through promising and delivering constancy, through 'being there', that children may find trust and security enough to work through some of their difficulties.

One observable feature of the best of these kinds of places is that they are so much about 'champions'. The concentration of vision, energy and determination to set up and maintain these kinds of services, often in the teeth of opposition, is a key ingredient in the success of organizations like Kids Company in London, or The Venture Playground in Wales. This kind of leadership is not replicable in any mundane sense, although many of its underlying principles are. Being child centred should mean just that – a place where children come first, where they can appear under their own steam, and once there, can rely on adults to be there for them, whatever the weather.

Conclusion

This book has set out in the clearest terms possible the impact of illegal drug use on families, but in conclusion, still leaves two key questions unanswered: can we help these families and will we help these families? I am clear in my own mind that we can help these families, even given the numbers of families involved, the intensity of the support they require and the length of time that support is likely to be needed. The question that follows is whether that help will be provided. At the level of current funding it is simply not going to be possible to support the numbers of families involved. However, this issue is considerably more complex than a matter of funding alone. In situations of often competing needs on the part of the drug user, children, grandparents, and siblings there has to be clarity in determining whose needs are to be given priority. It would be nice if we could come up with solutions that equally met each and everyone's needs but this is unlikely to be the case on more than a small number of occasions. If we are to learn anything at all from inquiries into the deaths of Caleb Ness and others, it ought to be the dangers of a divided focus that in effect divert attention away from the jeopardy. At present whilst policy makers and policy documents are talking clearly of the primacy of children's welfare, they are leaving service providers in a vacuum of inadequate guidance and oversight. Unless and until we can translate the aspirations of policy makers into the reality of service providers' interventions, all the fine words that may be uttered will still leave families having to find their own way through the chaos and the tragedy that is their loved one's drug use. If we fail to help these families successfully it should not be said that we did not know what they were going through.

References

ACMD (2003) 'Hidden Harm': Responding to the Needs of Children of Problem Drug Users; The Report of an Inquiry by the Advisory Council on the Misuse of Drugs. London: Home Office.

Alvarez, K.M., Donohue, B., Kenny, M.C., Cavanagh, N. and Romero, V. (2005) 'The process and consequences of reporting child maltreatment: a brief overview for professionals in the mental health field.' Aggression and Violent Behavior 10, 311–331.

Barnard, M. (2003) 'Between a rock and a hard place: the role of relatives in protecting children from the effects of parental drug problems.' Child and Family Social Work 8, 291–299.

Barnard, M. (2005a) 'Discomforting research: colliding moralities and looking for 'truth' in a study of parental drug problems.' Sociology of Health and Illness 27, 1, 1–19.

Barnard, M. (2005b) Drugs in the Family: The Impact on Parents and Siblings. York: Joseph Rowntree Foundation.

Barnard, M., Barlow, J., McKeganey, N., Hill, M. and Neale, J. (2000) 'Growing up in drug dependent households: parent, child and practitioner responses.' Reference no. K/OPR/2/2/D371. Chief Scientist Office of Scottish Executive.

Barnard, M. and Barlow, J. (2003) 'Discovering parental drug dependence: silence and disclosure.' Children and Society 17, 1, 45–56.

Barnard, M.A. and McKeganey, N.P. (2004) 'The impact of parental problem drug use on children: what is the problem and what can be done to help?' Addiction 99, 552–559.

Bauman, P.S. and Dougherty, F.E. (1983) 'Drug-addicted mothers' parenting and their children's development.' The International Journal of the Addictions 18, 291–302.

Bauman, P.S. and Levine, S.A. (1986) 'The development of children of drug addicts.' The International Journal of the Addictions 18, 291–302.

Bernstein, D.P., Stein, J.A., Newcomb, M.D., Walker, E., Pogge, D., Ahuluvalia, T., Stokes, J., Handelsman, L., Medrano, M., Desmond, D. and Zule, W. (2003) 'Development and validation of a brief screening version of the childhood trauma questionnaire.' Child Abuse and Neglect 27, 169–190.

Bluebond-Langner, M. (1996) In the Shadow of Illness: Parents and Siblings of the Chronically Ill Child. Princeton NJ: Princeton University Press.

Bowlby, J. (1969) Attachment. London: Hogarth Press.

Boyd, C. and Guthrie, B. (1996) 'Women, their significant others, and crack cocaine.' The American Journal of Addiction Psychiatry 5, 2, 156–166.

Brook, J., Whiteman, M., Gordon, A. and Brenden, C. (1983) 'Older brother's influence on younger sibling's drug use.' Journal of Psychology 114, 1, 83–90.

Brook, J., Whiteman, M., Gordon, A. and Brook, D. (1989) 'The role of older brothers in younger brothers' drug use viewed in the context of parent and peer influences.' The Journal of Genetic Psychology 151, 1, 59–75.

Brown-Standridge, F. (2000) 'Healing bittersweet legacies: revisiting contextual family therapy for grandparents raising children in crisis.' Journal of Marital and Family Therapy 26, 2, 185–197.

Buckley, H. (2000) 'Child protection: an unreflective practice.' Social Work Education 19, 3, 253–263.

Butler, R. and Bauld, L. (2005) 'The parents' experience: coping with drugs in the family.' Drugs: Education, Prevention and Policy 12, 1, 35–45.

Caliandro, G. and Hughes, C. (1998) 'The experience of being a grandmother who is the primary caregiver for her HIV positive grandchild.' Nursing Research 47, 2, 107–113.

Carlini-Marlatt, B. (2005) Grandparents in Custodial Care of Their Grandchildren. London: Mentor UK.

Catalano, R.F., Gainey, R.R., Fleming, C.B., Haggerty, K.P. and Johnson, N.O. (1999) 'An experimental intervention with families of substance abusers: one-year follow-up of the Focus on Family Project.' *Addiction 94*, 2, 241–254.

Chaffin, M., Kelleher, K. and Hollenberg, J. (1996) 'Onset of physical abuse and neglect: psychiatric substance abuse and social risk factors from social community data.' *Child Abuse and Neglect 20*, 191–203.

Chance, T. and Scannapieco, M. (2002) 'Ecological correlates of child maltreatment: similiarities and differences between child fatality and non-fatality cases.' *Child and Adolescent Social Work Journal 19*, 139–161.

Chase Goodman, C., Potts, M., Mayers Pasztor, E. and Scorzo, D. (2004) 'Grandmothers as kinship caregivers: private arrangements compared to public child welfare oversight.' *Children and Youth Services Review 26*, 287–305.

Child Welfare Information Gateway (2004) *Child Maltreatment 2002: Summary of Key Findings.* Washington: U.S. Department of Health and Human Services.

Child Welfare League of America (1998) *Alcohol and Other Drug Survey of State Child Welfare Agencies.* Washington: Child Welfare League of America.

Clark, D.B., Cornelius, J.R., Kirisci, L. and Tarter, R.E. (2005) 'Childhood risk categories for adolescent substance involvement: a general liability typology.' *Drug and Alcohol Dependence 77*, 1, 13–21.

Clark, D.B., Cornelius, J.R., Wood, D.S. and Vanyukov, M. (2004) 'Psychopathology risk transmission in children of parents with substance use disorders.' *American Journal of Psychiatry 161*, 4, 685–691.

Connell-Carrick, K. (2003) 'A critical review of the empirical literature: identifying correlates of child neglect.' *Child and Adolescent Social Work Journal 20*, 5, 389–425.

Coohey, C. (2003) 'Making judgements about risk in substantiated cases of supervisory neglect.' *Child Abuse and Neglect 27*, 7, 821–840.

Copello, A. and Orford, J. (2002) 'Addiction and the family: is it time for services to take notice of the evidence?' *Addiction 97*, 11, 1361–1363.

Corcoran, J. (2000) 'Family interventions with child physical abuse and neglect: a critical review.' *Children and Services Review 22*, 563–591.

Cornelius, J.R., Clark, D.B., Weyant, R., Bretz, W., Corby, P., Mezzich, A. and Kirsci, L. (2004) 'Dental abnormalities in children of fathers with substance use disorders.' *Addictive Behaviors 29*, 5, 979–982.

Cramer, J.C. and Bell McDonald, K. (1996) 'Kin support and family stress: two sides to early childbearing and support networks.' *Human Organization 55*, 160–169.

Department of Health (1989) Children Act 1989. London: HMSO.

Department of Health (1995) *Children (Scotland) Act 1995.* London: HMSO.

Dingwall, R., Eekelaar, J. and Murray, T. (1983) *The Protection of Children: State Intervention and Family Life.* Oxford: Blackwell.

Dingwall, R. and Robinson, K. (1993) 'Policing the family? Health visiting and the public surveillance of private behaviour.' In A. Beattie, M. Gott, L. Jones and M. Sidell (eds) *Health and Wellbeing: A Reader.* Basingstoke: Macmillan.

Duncan, T., Alpert, A., Duncan, S. and Hops, H. (1996) 'Multilevel covariance structure analysis of sibling substance use and interfamily conflict.' *Journal of Psychopathology and Behavioural Assessment 18*, 4, 347–369.

Ferguson, H. (2005) 'Working with violence, the emotions and the pyscho-social dynamics of child protection: reflections on the Victoria Climbié Case.' *Social Work Education 24*, 7, 781–795.

Forrester, D. (2000) 'Parental substance misuse and child protection in a British sample: a survey of children on the Child Protection Register in an Inner London district office.' *Child Abuse Review 9*, 235–246.

Gerace, L.M., Camilleri, D. and Ayres, L. (1993) 'Sibling perspectives on schizophrenia and the family.' *Schizophrenia Bulletin 19*, 3, 637–647.

Goodman, G., Hans, S. and Cox, S. (1999) 'Attachment behaviour and its antecedents in offspring born to methadone maintained women.' *Journal of Clinical Psychology 28*, 58–69.

Harwin, J. and Forrester, D. (2002) 'Parental substance misuse and child welfare: a study of social work with families in which parents misuse drugs or alcohol.' London: Interim Report for Nuffield Foundation.

Hawley, T.L., Halle, T.G., Drasin, R.E. and Thomas, N.G. (1995) 'Children of addicted mothers: effects of the 'crack epidemic' on the caregiving environment and the development of preschoolers.' *American Journal of Orthopsychiatry 65*, 3, 364–379.

Hay, G., Gannon, M., McKeganey, N., Hutchinson, S. and Goldberg, D. (2005) *Estimating the National and Local Prevalence of Problem Drug Use in Scotland.* Edinburgh: Scottish Executive.

Hien, D. and Honeyman, T. (2000) 'A closer look at the drug abuse–maternal aggression link.' *Journal of Interpersonal Violence 15*, 5, 503–522.

Hogan, D. and Higgins, L. (2001) *When Parents Use Drugs: Key Findings from a Study of Children in the Care of Drug Using Parents.* Trinity College, Dublin: The Children's Research Centre.

Howe, D. (2005) *Child Abuse and Neglect: Attachment, Development and Intervention.* Basingstoke: Palgrave Macmillan.

Huberty, D. and Huberty, C. (1986) 'Sabotaging siblings: an overlooked aspect of family therapy with drug dependent adolescents.' *Journal of Psychoactive Drugs 18*, 1, 31–41.

Jaudes, P.K. and Ekwo, E. (1995) 'Association of drug abuse and child abuse.' *Child Abuse and Neglect 19*, 9, 1065–1075.

Jendrek Platt, M. (1993) 'Grand Parents who Parent their Grandchildren: effects on lifestyle.' *Journal of Marriage and the Family 55*, 609–621.

Johnson, J., Boney, T. and Brown, B. (1991) 'Evidence of depressive symptoms in children of substance abusers.' *International Journal of Addictions 25*, 4a, 465–479.

Jones, M. and Jones, D. (2000) 'The contagious nature of antisocial behavior.' *Criminology 38*, 1, 25–47.

Kandel, D.B. (1990) 'Parenting styles, drug use, and children's adjustment in families of young adults.' *Journal of Marriage and the Family 52*, 183–196.

Kelleher, K., Chaffin, M., Hollenberg, J. and Fischer, E. (1994) 'Alcohol and drug disorders among physically abusive and neglectful parents in a community based sample.' *American Journal of Public Health 84*, 1586–1590.

Kelley, S.J. (1993) 'Caregiver stress in grandparents raising grandchildren.' *Image: Journal of Nursing Scholarship 25*, 4, 331–337.

Kerwin, M. (2005) 'Collaboration between child welfare and substance abuse fields: combined treatment programs for mothers.' *Journal of Pediatric Psychology 30*, 7, 581–597.

Knisely, J.S., Barker, S.B., Ingersoll, K.S. and Dawson, K.S. (2000) 'Psychopathology in substance abusing women reporting childhood sexual abuse.' *Journal of Addictive Diseases 19*, 31–44.

Kolar, A.F., Brown, B.S., Haertzen, C.A. and Michaelson, B.S. (1994) 'Children of substance abusers: the life experiences of children of opiate addicts in methadone maintenance.' *American Journal of Drug and Alcohol Abuse 20*, 2, 159–171.

Kroll, B. and Taylor, A. (2003) *Parental Substance Misuse and Child Welfare.* London: Jessica Kingsley Publishers.

Lalayants, M. and Epstein, I. (2005) 'Evaluating multidisciplinary child abuse and neglect teams: a research agenda.' *Child Welfare 84*, 4, 433–458.

Lamorey, S. (1999) *Parentification of Siblings of Children With Disability or Chronic Disease.* California: Sage, 1000 Oaks.

Liddle, H.A., Dakof, G.A., Parker, K., Diamond, G.S., Barett, K. and Tejada, M. (2001) 'Multidimensional family therapy for adolescent substance abuse: results of a randomised clinical trial.' *American Journal of Drug and Alcohol Abuse 27*, 4, 651–688.

Locke, T.F. and Newcomb, M.D. (2003) 'Childhood maltreatment, parental alcohol/drug related problems and global parental dysfunction.' *Professional Psychology: Research and Practice 34*, 73–79.

Lord Laming (2003) *The Victoria Climbié Inquiry: Report of an Inquiry.* London: Home Office.

Luthar, S., Merikangas, K. and Rounsaville, B. (1993) 'Parental psychopathology and disorders in offspring – a study of relatives of drug users.' *Journal of Nervous and Mental Disease 181*, 6, 351–357.

McIntosh, J. and McKeganey, N. (2001) *Beating the Dragon: The Recovery from Dependent Drug Use.* London: Prentice Hall.

McKeganey, N. and Barnard, M. (2002) *Sex Work on the Streets: Prostitutes and Their Clients.* Milton Keynes: Open University Press.

McKeganey, N., Barnard, M. and McIntosh, J. (2002) 'Paying the price for their parent's addiction: meeting the needs of the children of drug using parents.' *Drugs: Education, Prevention and Policy 9,* 3, 233–246.

Minkler, M., Roe, K.M. and Price, M. (1992) 'The physical and emotional health of grandmothers raising grandchildren in the crack cocaine epidemic.' *Gerontological Society of America 32,* 6, 752–761.

Minkler, M., Roe, K.M. and Roe, M. (1993) *Grandmothers as Caregivers: Raising Children of the Crack Cocaine Epidemic.* London: Sage.

Moss, H.B., Lynch, K.G. and Hardie, T.L. (2003) 'Affiliation with deviant peers among children of substance dependent fathers from pre-adolescence into adolescence: associations with problem behaviours.' *Drug and Alcohol Dependence 71,* 117–125.

Mountenay, J. (1998) *Children of Drug Using Parents.* London: Highlight, National Children's Bureau.

Murphy, J.M., Jellinek, M., Quinn, D., Smith, G., Poitrast, F.G. and Goshko, M. (1991) 'Substance abuse and serious child maltreatment: prevalence, risk and outcome in a court sample.' *Child Abuse and Neglect 15,* 197–211.

Nair, P., Schuler, M.E., Black, M.M., Kettinger, L. and Harrington, D. (2003) 'Cumulative environmental risk in substance abusing women: early intervention, parenting stress, child abuse potential and child development.' *Child Abuse and Neglect 27,* 997–1017.

Neale, J. (1999) 'Experiences of illicit drug overdose: an ethnographic study of emergency hospital attendances.' *Contemporary Drug Problems 26,* 505–530.

Needle, R., McCubbin, H., Wilson, M., Reineck, R., Lazar, A. and Mederer, H. (1986) 'Interpersonal influences in adolescent drug use – the role of older siblings, parents, and peers.' *International Journal of the Addictions 21,* 7, 739–766.

Nurco, D. (1999) 'Early deviance and related risk factors in the children of narcotic addicts.' *American Journal of Drug and Alcohol Abuse 25,* 25–45.

O'Brien, S., Hammond, H. and McKinnon, M. (2003) *Report of the Caleb Ness Inquiry.* Edinburgh: Edinburgh and Lothians Child Protection Committee.

O'Flynn, M. (1999) 'The Adoption and Safe Families Act of 1997: changing child welfare policy without addressing parental substance abuse.' *Journal of Contemporary Health Law and Policy 16,* 243–271.

Ohannessian, C.M., Hesselbrock, V.M., Kramer, J., Bucholz, K., Schuckit, M., Kuperman, S. and Nurnberger, J.L. Jr. (2004) 'Parental substance use consequences and adolescent psychopathology.' *Journal of Studies on Alcohol 65,* 6, 725–730.

Orford, J., Natera, G., Davies, J., Nava, A., Mora, J., Rigby, K., Bradbury, D., Copello, A. and Velleman, R. (1998a) 'Tolerate, engage or withdraw: a study of the structure of families coping with alcohol and drug problems at home: findings from Mexican and English families.' *Addiction 93,* 1799–1813.

Orford, J., Natera, G., Davies, J., Nava, A., Mora, J., Rigby, A., Bradbury, C., Copello, A. and Velleman, R. (1998b) 'Stresses and strains for family members.' *Salud Mental 5,* 1, 1–13.

Orford, J., Natera, G., Velleman, R., Copello, A., Bowie, N., Bradbury, C., Davies, J., Mora, J., Nava, A., Rigby, K. and Tiburcio, M. (2001) 'Ways of coping and the health of relatives facing drug and alcohol problems in Mexico and England.' *Addiction 96,* 761–774.

Ornoy, A., Michailevskaya, V., Lukashov, I., Bar-Hamburger, R. and Harel, S. (1996) 'The developmental outcome of children born into heroin-dependent mothers, raised at home or adopted.' *Child Abuse and Neglect 20,* 5, 385–396.

Porowski, A., Burgdorf, K. and Herrell, J. (2004) 'Effectiveness and sustainability of residential substance abuse treatment programs for pregnant and parenting women.' *Evaluation and Program Planning 27,* 191–198.

Reder, P., Duncan, S. and Gray, M. (2003) *Beyond Blame: Child Abuse Tragedies Revisited.* London: Routledge.

Ridener Gottwald, S. and Thurman, S.K. (1994) 'The effects of prenatal cocaine exposure on mother–infant interaction and arousal in the newborn period.' *Topics in Early Childhood Special Education 14,* 217–231.

Roe, K.M., Minkler, M., Barnwell, R.-S. and Jendrek, P.M. (1994) 'The assumption of caregiving: grandmothers raising the children of the crack cocaine epidemic.' *Qualitative Health Research 4*, 3, 281–303.

Roizen, N.J., Blondis, T.A. and Irwin, M. (1996) 'Psychiatric and developmental disorders in families of children with Attention Deficit Hyperactivity Disorder.' *Archives of Pediatric Adolescent Medicine 150*, 203–208.

Schuler, M., Nair, P., Black, M.M. and Kettinger, L. (2000) 'Mother–infant Interaction: effects of a home intervention and ongoing maternal drug use.' *Journal of Clinical Child Psychology 29*, 3, 424–431.

Scottish Executive (2003) *Getting our Priorities Right: Policy and Practice Guidelines for Working with Children and Families Affected by Problem Drug Use.* Edinburgh: Scottish Executive.

Semidei, J., Radel, L. and Nolan, C. (2001) 'Substance abuse and child welfare: clear linkages and promising responses.' *Child Welfare League of America 80*, 2, 109–128.

Shulman, L., Shapira, S. and Hirshfield, S. (2000) 'Outreach development services to children of patients in treatment for substance abuse.' *American Journal of Public Health 90*, 12, 1930–1933.

Silverman, K. and Schonberg, A. (2001) 'Adolescent children of drug abusing parents.' *Adolescent Medicine State of the Art Reviews 12*, 3, 485–491.

Smith, B.D. and Testa, M.F. (2002) 'The risk of subsequent maltreatment allegations in families with substance-exposed infants.' *Child Abuse and Neglect 26*, 97–114.

Social Work Inspection Agency (2005) *An Inspection into the Care and Protection of Children in Eilean Sar.* Edinburgh: Scottish Executive.

Stevenson, O. (1998) *Neglected Children: Issues and Dilemmas.* Oxford: Blackwell.

Suchman, N.E. and Luthar, S.S. (2000) 'Maternal addiction, child maladjustment and socio-demographic risks: implication for parenting behaviours.' *Addiction 95*, 9, 1417–1428.

Taylor, A. and Kroll, B. (2004) 'Working with parental substance misuse: dilemmas for practice.' *British Journal of Social Work 34*, 8, 1115–1132.

Terling, T. (1999) 'The efficacy of family reunification practices: reentry rates and correlates of reentry for abused and neglected children reunited with their families.' *Child Abuse and Neglect 23*, 12, 1359–1370.

Usher, K., Jackson, D. and O'Brien, L. (2005) 'Adolescent drug abuse: helping families survive.' *International Journal of Mental Health Nursing 14*, 3, 209–214.

Vakalahi, H. (2001) 'Adolescent substance use and family-based risk and protective factors: a literature review.' *Journal of Drug Education 31*, 1, 29–46.

Velleman, R. and Templeton, L. (2003) 'Alcohol, drugs and the family: results from a long-running research programme within the UK.' *European Addiction Research 9*, 103–112.

Watson, H. and Levine, J. (1989) 'Psychotherapy and mandated reporting of child abuse.' *American Journal of Orthopsychiatry 59*, 246–256.

Weinstein, B., Levine, J., Kogan, M., Harkavy-Friedman, J. and Miller, M. (2000) *Child Abuse and Neglect 24*, 10, 1317–1328.

Weissman, M.M., McAvay, G., Goldstein, R.B., Nunes, E.V., Verdeli, H. and Wickramaratne, P.J. (1999) 'Risk/protective factors among addicted mothers' offspring: a replication study.' *American Journal of Drug and Alcohol Abuse 25*, 4, 661–679.

Wilens, T.E., Hahesy, A.L., Biederman, J., Bredin, E., Tanguay, S., Kwon, A. and Faraone, S.V. (2005) 'Influence of parental SUD and ADHD on ADHD in their offspring: preliminary results from a pilot-controlled family study.' *American Journal on Addictions 14*, 179–187.

Williams, R.J. and Chang, S.Y. (2000) 'A comprehensive and comparative review of adolescent substance abuse treatment outcomes.' *Clinical Psychology: Science and Practice 7*, 2, 138–166.

Subject Index

Author Index

ACMD 13, 17, 135, 139
Alvarez, K.M. 158, 159
Ayres, L. 14

Barlow, J. 22–3
Barnard, M. 14, 21–3, 60, 61, 68,
     81, 101, 116, 120
Bauld, L. 13
Bauman, P.S. 16, 19
Bell McDonald, K. 17
Bernstein, D.P. 15
Blondis, T.A. 20
Bluebond-Langner, M. 14, 45
Boney, T. 19
Bowlby, J. 16
Boyd, C. 18
Brook, J. 19
Brown, B. 19
Brown-Standridge, F. 18
Buckley, H. 136, 140
Burgdorf, K. 15
Butler, R. 13

Caliandro, G. 17
Camilleri, D. 14
Carlini-Marlatt, B. 17, 18
Catalano, R.F. 162
Chaffin, M. 14
Chance, T. 15, 60
Chang, S.Y. 154
Chase Goodman, C. 17, 18
Child Welfare Information
     Gateway 14
Child Welfare League
     of America 15
Clark, D.B. 20, 100
Connell-Carrick, K. 15, 16
Coohey, C. 72
Copello, A. 13
Corcoran, J. 15
Cornelius, J.R. 15
Cox, S. 16
Cramer, J.C. 17

Dingwall, R. 138, 140, 146, 150
Dougherty, F.E. 16, 19
Duncan, S. 136
Duncan, T. 19, 121

Eekelaar, J. 140
Ekwo, E. 15
Epstein, I. 146

Ferguson, H. 159
Forrester, D. 15

Gerace, L.M. 14
Goodman, G. 16
Gray, M. 136
Guthrie, B. 18

Hammond, H. 136
Hans, S. 16
Hardie, T.L. 20
Harwin, J. 15
Hawley, T.L. 14
Hay, G. 21
Herrell, J. 15
Hien, D. 17
Higgins, L. 14
Hirshfield, S. 15
Hogan, D. 14
Hollenberg, J. 14
Honeyman, T. 17
Howe, D. 80, 97
Huberty, C. 13, 44
Huberty, D. 13, 44
Hughes, C. 17

Irwin, M. 20

Jackson, D. 25
Jaudes, P.K. 15
Johnson, J. 19
Jones, D. 19
Jones, M. 19

Kandel, D.B. 16, 19
Kelleher, K. 14, 15
Kelley, S.J. 17
Kerwin, M. 16
Knisely, J.S. 19
Kolar, A.F. 17, 20, 87
Kroll, B. 15, 137, 143, 146

Lalayants, M. 146
Laming, Lord 156
Lamorey, S. 14
Levine, J. 159
Levine, S.A. 16, 19, 159
Liddle, H.A. 154
Locke, T.F. 14
Luthar, S. 16, 18
Lynch, K.G. 20

McIntosh, J. 14, 50, 71, 79
McKeganey, N. 14, 18, 50, 68,
     71, 79
McKinnon, M. 136
Merikangas, K. 18
Minkler, M. 18, 102
Moss, H.B. 20
Mountenay, J. 156
Murphy, J.M. 15
Murray, T. 140

Nair, P. 15
Neale, J. 95
Needle, R. 19
Newcomb, M.D. 14
Nolan, C. 15
Nurco, D. 20

O'Brien, L. 25
O'Brien, S. 136, 142
O'Flynn, M. 158
Ohannessian, C.M. 20
Orford, J. 13
Ornoy, A. 18, 160

Porowski, A. 15
Price, M. 18
Pullman, P. 61

Radel, L. 15
Reder, P. 136, 150
Ridener Gottwald, S. 16
Robinson, K. 138
Roe, K.M. 18, 102
Roe, M. 102
Roizen, N.J. 20
Rounsaville, B. 18

Scannapieco, M. 15, 60
Schonberg, A. 19
Schuler, M. 16
Scottish Executive 22, 139
Semidei, J. 15, 158
Shapira, S. 15
Shulman, L. 15
Silverman, K. 19
Smith, B.D. 15
Social Work Inspection
     Agency 142
Stevenson, O. 136
Suchman, N.E. 16

Taylor, A. 15, 137, 143, 146
Templeton, L. 13
Terling, T. 15
Testa, M.F. 15
Thurman, S.K. 16

Usher, K. 25

Vakalahi, H. 19, 121
Velleman, R. 13

Watson, H. 159
Weinstein, B. 159
Weissman, M.M. 19
Wilens, T.E. 20
Williams, R.J. 154